1ST **JOB** SERIES.com
JOB SEEKER

How To Get Your First And Build The Career You Want

Over <u>100 tips and hints</u> and a clear practical step by step guide to finding your first job and building on it to achieve an amazing career

Angela Middleton

How To Get Your First Job

First published in 2015 by

Panoma Press Ltd
St Vincent Drive, St Albans, Herts, AL1 5SJ, UK
info@panomapress.com
www.panomapress.com

Book layout by Neil Coe.

Printed on acid-free paper from managed forests.

ISBN 978-1-909623-88-0

This book is available online and in bookstores.

**Printed and bound in Great Britain by
TJ International Ltd, Padstow, Cornwall**

Dedication and Acknowledgement

This book has taken me a year to write, while trying to balance all the everyday demands that come with having a family and a very busy business! I feel grateful that I have been able to learn so much about this subject through my work and thankful to everyone who has supported me and contributed in various ways to enable me to complete this book.

Thank you to my lovely children Stephen and Annabel who have shared with me their hopes and dreams for their own careers; to my husband Steve for his unending support; to my parents for inspiring my own work ethic; to my fantastic team at MiddletonMurray who extend advice to young people every day and work tirelessly to get the best opportunities for them and who contributed many of the great case studies contained within the book; to my trusted test readers (Joy Lamina, Steve Sutherland, Alison Colwell, Matthew Brown, Leigh Christodoulou, Ben Mason, Anthea Bloom, Dawn Mason, Julia Hopwood, James Brokenshire, Jackie Oliver, Fatai Oseni) for providing such great input; to my Assistant Jenny Shepherd for supporting me and ensuring my writing time was diarised no matter what! To Mindy and her team at Panoma Press for guiding me to bring this book to life; to all the small businesses that have worked with us to give young people their first job, and most of all to the thousands of young people, their parents and their advisors, who have trusted me and my company to help them start their careers.

This book is dedicated to all of you with my sincere best wishes that your own careers continue to flourish and that together we can continue to help many more young people launch great careers too.

· Testimonials

"MiddletonMurray have a really great understanding of the needs of their local young people, local businesses and their local communities. They also totally keep in focus that the aim of traineeships and apprenticeships is to get the right young person into the right job - Angela's book highlights perfectly why they've been so successful."

Tessa Oversby FCIPD ACIB – Head of Employability, LifeSkills, Personal & Corporate Banking, Barclays Bank

"I have seen at first hand how successful MiddletonMurray are at getting young people into apprenticeships and then full time employment. The techniques they deploy, as outlined in this book by Angela, are innovative and effective and are providing opportunities for significant numbers of young people to take their first step on the jobs ladder."

Peter Varney – CEO KEH Sport Ltd & Vice Chairman, Ebbsfleet United FC

"Crammed with an incredible amount of really useful information… a great reference point and guide to help the young job applicant secure the post they are looking for."

James Brokenshire – MP for Old Bexley and Sidcup

"A clear strategic step-by-step guide to finding employment."

Dawn Mason – Safeguarding Manager at MiddletonMurray

"This will motivate, inspire and give you the
confidence to achieve your goals."

Anthea Bloom – Parent

"Angela Middleton's *How To Get Your First Job….And Build The
Career You Want* is an extremely engaging and informative book
that is loaded with proven techniques, practical ideas and
strategies to help young people make those first, very important
steps on the career ladder. Packed with great tips from an industry
expert, this book should be treated as your personal manual for
career success."

Steve Sutherland – Sports Marketing Consultant

"From reading this book *How To Get Your First Job… And Build
The Career You Want* I feel that if I was still a student at secondary
school going into my last year of GCSEs I would have been more
prepared to face the world of work, knowing how to stand out at
interviews, and the depth of research one has to do in order to
increase your chances of success. This is a golden nugget that all
students should have tucked away in their school bag ready to pull
out and use."

Leigh Christodoulou – Trainer at MiddletonMurray

"This book will inspire countless young people to go for it!"

**Matthew Brown – Head Teacher,
Blackfen School for Girls**

"An informative and interesting twist on modern job hunting."

**Julia Hopwood – Information and Guidance Manager
at MiddletonMurray**

Introduction and Foreword

- This book will help you get your first job – and even your next job if you have one already – but only if you adopt a disciplined approach and take it step-by-step, coming back to this book at regular intervals rather than trying to do it all at once. Of course you can read the book all in one go initially but then I would recommend you pick it up and put it down as you work through each item, returning and re-reading relevant sections to aid the completion of the Action Plan steps before moving to the next.

- There are three parts to this book: Part 1 Preparation, Part 2 Action, Part 3 Tools.

- There are 14 chapters.

- Within each chapter there are many pieces of advice that can be read in isolation and which can be used as an aide memoire if you do not want to read the whole book – or preferably for referral once you have! There are currently 120 of these so I hope this book can be seen as a book of hints and tips for you too.

- There are 20 steps which if followed will create a comprehensive and updateable Action Plan for you online. There is a module on our website that you can use in conjunction with the book. All you need to do is log on to www.1stjobseries.com, sign up, and then you can download any of the templates you wish.

- If you find this book a bit daunting, please try not to worry about all the steps and tips at the same time. Just start with the first chapter, the first step and the first action and then continue working through these bit by bit.

- You might also want to read it with your parents, friends or teachers who can help you carry out some of the actions suggested.

- This book is aimed at everyone, including those who have zero qualifications and experience and who just want a good job. It is not just for those who want high-profile careers although it certainly provides a springboard for you to achieve that if it's what you want.

- Many readers will be tempted to jump straight to the third section of this book – the Tools. In a way this really is the least important part because you can find templates of CVs and interview questions anywhere on the internet. This section really is here for completeness rather than anything else; it is the first two sections of the book that will have most impact and get you the best results, not the tools. Therefore I would urge you to read those first and as a priority. The third section containing tools is for you to use once you have understood sections one and two on Preparation and Action.

- In this book you will find numerous case studies of people just like you who adopted the strategy and followed the steps in this book and got the result they wanted. In these cases, we just guided them through the steps. They are proof that this works!

Contents

PART 1
PREPARATION

Chapter 1

The Landscape in the UK – It's Never Too Soon – There's Never Been More Opportunity

Jobs are everywhere!

There are jobs literally everywhere and no one needs to be unemployed in the UK today. This may appear to be a bold statement and you may not believe this to be true because there are so many people out of work, however as you continue to read this section you will see that this is indeed the case.

The trouble is that this does not match the perception of young people today. When I speak to school and college leavers they unanimously believe that it will be difficult to get a job, even before they've started looking. And when they don't get the first job they apply for, it reinforces that belief and often they stop trying or at least their enthusiasm is dramatically reduced. This belief is also often reinforced by the beliefs and experiences of their friends and their family members.

In my years as a recruiter, running businesses that prepare people for different careers and places them into jobs, I have seen that the reality is very different. No matter what is happening in the economy – and even throughout the recession – I have witnessed literally thousands of times that there is a technique in finding a great job – not just any job but a fantastic start leading to a fulfilling and impressive career. We have developed this technique over the years to a point where I can literally define the steps that you need to take, and if you do take them I can guarantee you will achieve a great outcome. If you are sceptical and don't believe me, I have proof! In the last three years, during one of the most difficult economic times in UK history, we have placed over 1,000 young people who came to us disillusioned, into great jobs. And once they start in that first job they never look back and I am delighted to be able to keep in touch with them and watch their progress. We have case studies galore of people just like you who have come to us having applied for many jobs they say, and within six weeks we have had them into work. This ranges from 16-year-olds with no qualifications through to 24-year-olds with strong degrees. We placed a 16-year-old who wanted to get into advertising in a top media agency and a 23-year-old graduate who wanted to become a corporate banker in a leading bank as an investment analyst. At the back of this book you will see many testimonials so I hope that is enough to convince you that I know what I am saying to be true and that if you follow my steps you will achieve the same outcome for yourself.

So knowing all this makes it very frustrating for me to see so many young people disillusioned and unemployed when I *know* they needn't be – no matter what qualifications or experience they lack. I therefore decided to write this book – which is really more like a manual – to help young people like you who are aged between 16 and 24 and have anything from zero qualifications to a Master's degree and very little work experience to get their first step on their career ladder. The book provides full details on exactly what you have to do to get your first job or your next job if you have already had one or currently have one that you don't like.

I have also produced an Action Plan online, which you can use in conjunction with this book. At the end of each step in this book I will ask you to go to your Action Plan and update it with what I have shown you. My aim is that by the end of the book you will have a personalised Action Plan ready for you to *implement* – and if you do then I *guarantee* that three months from now you will have a great new job and be on your way to building your career.

The word *guarantee* is a strong one – but so is the word *if* and so is the word *implement*. I can *guarantee* you a great outcome but only *if* you *implement* the steps I outline. Some of the steps are more difficult than others and might appear a bit daunting initially but every single one of them is within your ability, control and power. Great jobs never fall into anyone's lap – they never have and they never will. When we hear stories of how someone just happened to be in the right place at the right time to land an amazing new job or promotion, there's nearly always a story behind it of how that person came to be in that place. And usually the story is that they have worked hard to build up to that point. So, in order to get the best from this book you need to be prepared to go on a journey – read the advice, follow the directions, and you will achieve what you want.

Step 1 – You can find the Action Plan at at www.1stjobseries. com – go there now to set it up, then return back here to continue.

Published vacancies

There is unemployment in all types of economy. Even in the depths of recession in 2009/10 we saw people getting new jobs all the time, and even in the real boom of 2007 we saw people struggling to get jobs. There is no need therefore to blame the recession on your difficulties in getting a good job – it's just how it always is. There are literally over a million live jobs advertised in the UK today and they can be found in a variety of places. I will talk about some of those places here.

Recruitment agencies are one rich source. There are around 8,000 of them throughout the UK specialising in all sorts of roles and sectors. They recruit on behalf of companies (we'll call them employers) who either don't have the time or the skills or both to recruit their own staff and who prefer to outsource this to an agency. Agencies usually only get paid by companies once the new person is in the job. The job seeker is not the person who pays. Therefore it is very much in the interests of the recruitment consultants who work in agencies to choose a good candidate who will shine in the role, so the employer is happy and pays the agency the fee. Bearing this in mind, it's in your interest to build relationships with certain agencies that have the jobs and connections with employers that you want. I will speak more about this in Chapter 6.

Job boards are another source of vacancies. There are hundreds of job boards in the UK including some privately owned ones and also some government run ones; one million jobs are advertised on these at any one time. Often the jobs placed on them are from agencies, which is how you find out which agencies to talk to, but also often by the employers themselves who don't want to use agencies. Job boards are like a big screening place and can be used in two ways. Firstly you can apply directly for jobs by following the instructions and sending your CV, covering letter etc. Sometimes they just ask you to call them. The other way is to load your CV on to the job board itself and fill in an online questionnaire about what you are seeking and then every time a new job is added that fulfils your criteria you will get an email. Before you know it you get tons of emails with new jobs on! A full list of agencies and job boards is found at www.1stjobseries.com

Large employers also have their own job boards so once you have decided which companies you would like to work for, you can go on to their site and search for and apply for jobs in the same way that you would a job board.

Social media is another great source of jobs. If you just Google 'vacancies' tons of vacancies will come up and if you go on to LinkedIn and Twitter and search for jobs you will be amazed how many vacancies will come up there too. You can apply for those and/or connect with the individuals and companies advertising them so you can develop those relationships as part of your network building.

Also the press – newspapers, industry magazines etc. will advertise new roles.

So as you can see, there are a huge number of live jobs right now that are being advertised. However, you may think, many of those are not for you and require skills or experience or qualifications you don't have. You are right, but many of them *are* for you and by using my techniques you will learn how to find those ones. This leads me on to the world of hidden vacancies.

The world of hidden vacancies

There are more 'hidden' vacancies than there are visible vacancies. What do I mean by this? Well, as a recruiter we see these emerge all day every day from a variety of sources. For example, large companies that run programmes for young people put in place extremely stringent selection criteria and, as a result, they often cannot fill their allocation. What they then do, right at the last minute, is loosen those criteria, and suddenly where there were no vacancies for you, they then reappear! With smaller companies – companies with fewer than 100 or so staff – they tend to be under great pressure because they are growing and you often find that managers have several sets of responsibilities. In these companies they are often desperate to share the load with new entrants, however they never get round to advertising for these roles because they are too busy. It's only when someone with drive and enthusiasm presents themselves that the company owner will suddenly decide that yes they would like to take that person on, and suddenly there is a vacancy no one knew about. Sometimes these roles aren't 'proper' roles at first; they are called things like work experience placements, traineeships or internships – but I very rarely, if ever, see a situation where the young person is good and shines and yet doesn't get taken on permanently.

Another source of hidden vacancies is for graduates. Many graduates believe that they have to go in via a graduate scheme. So often we see this is not the case. They can enter into an entry level position, even a temporary position, and then once in, prove they are good enough and get switched to the graduate scheme.

Temporary positions via agencies are a good source too. Often we see people take a quite mundane temporary role just to get some money and experience, and then once in the job they are the first to find out about a potential new vacancy and they get it before it's advertised. Or they shine in their temporary role and it's made permanent and they start working their way up. We see this so much. For example, one of our graduate applicants Colin secured temporary work through my recruitment company and is now working for that company full-time. We often see him in our town, he is happy and seems to be building a nice career for himself after searching for a long time.

Finally, interviews for one job can turn into interviews for several other different roles. Again we often see this where two people go for a role and the employer decides to take both on.

These are just a few examples of hidden jobs. I am sure you will be surprised to know that between 2011 and 2014 we placed over 1,000 16–19-year-olds into companies where before we suggested the idea to the employer, there was no vacancy!

Timing – it's never too soon or too late to start

When I speak to year 11s, 12s, 13s or even graduates in their first year, I always emphasise a key message: "It's never too soon to be seeking your first job." Just because you have another couple of years of A levels or degree study ahead of you does not mean it's not essential to achieve a great work experience or internship placement over the holidays to set you up for getting a great job when you do actually leave school or college or university. If you are in this situation you do indeed have a bright future but that future is much closer than you think! By getting a relevant placement while on holiday you demonstrate your work ethic and industry interest to an employer very early on, and this can sometimes shortcut the job seeking process when you leave and save you from having to start from scratch competing with the crowds who are job seeking after the leaving dates and everything becomes a lot harder. For example, Alice secured an internship with KPMG while she was still doing her A levels. She did well, and when she reapplied in her last year of university she secured a full-time position with them. In fact they even agreed to hold the job open for her so she could take a gap year before joining them!

Having said that, it's never too late! It's amazing how many young people I meet aged 23–24 and even younger who feel they are written off and have missed the boat for all the best jobs. Absolute nonsense! We see people all the time who are disillusioned because they have done a series of dead end jobs and cannot seem to start a career. Well, if we look at it in perspective, even those people have around 50 years of working life left, and once you put it like that it really makes little difference if you are 21 or 24. The important thing is to recognise where you are and what you have to do to get where you want to be. Usually the answer to that is to get more relevant work experience and also to achieve more qualifications. This all takes time but this is crucially important, right? Therefore what could be more important? Education and study should really be a lifetime commitment; I see people who have had several careers during their lives and have trained for them all separately at different stages. So committing to some more qualifications and training at this point is imperative if it's needed. The same goes for unpaid work experience if that is missing. There are a variety of Government funded schemes to assist you in these areas and you can find these on www.1stjobseries.com

Government incentives

Finally, timing is never an issue for young people because the Government in the UK is very well aware of the importance of developing skills for young people and introducing them to the labour market no matter what the state of the economy. If there is a recession this is even more true and we often see schemes where, for example, they actually pay small companies a grant to create apprenticeship opportunities for young people or to upskill existing staff or to take on unemployed people. They also make it a condition when they award large contracts to large companies in all sectors and industries that a certain number of new apprentices must be taken on. All this information is in the public domain so you can research who's just won a big contract and then contact them for new opportunities.

Chapter 2

Things Within Us That Help Us Succeed or Stop Us Succeeding – Be An Implementer!

The best qualified, most lucky and connected people don't get the best jobs!

People who cannot get a job can often be fantastic at coming up with reasons why this is. Reasons given include a lack of skills, experience or qualifications. It can be blamed on bad luck or lack of connections; sometimes they may say they don't have any friends in high places or they might blame the economy. What I rarely see is people blaming it on their own behaviours, as if this is not a factor in the equation, and if they do then they will often tell me that they have applied for thousands of jobs. Once I delve a bit deeper, this almost always turns out not to be true, or if it is, the applications have not been carried out in the most effective way, i.e. for each job application they have not sent a CV then followed that up with a call then followed up a second and numerous times until such time as they have received a rejection and some feedback.

I have seen many people with less experience and fewer skills, contacts and qualifications secure better jobs than those who have more of all those things. Why is this?

Well, over the years of observing this I have seen that this is due to behaviours and job search activity – nothing else. And the key behaviour that exhibits itself time and time again is persistence and implementation. Those who have become totally obsessed with finding their job, who listen to advice, and most important of all then *implement* it repeatedly, are the ones who are successful. Of course, qualifications are extremely important and can often be a deciding factor but even more often we see that behaviours make the difference.

If you look at the other factors in securing a job, they just don't get the same results. Let's look at connections. These just might open doors for you and I myself have used connections before to get someone an introduction and even a first interview. However, usually that is where it stops. A connection can open the door but it cannot keep it open. If the candidate does not perform well in interview then no amount of connection will secure them the job.

Then there is luck. Many believe if you are lucky then a job might land in your lap. However, I have seen this work very differently. I am a firm believer in the 'you have to be in it to win it' school of thought. This means that if you are going to do enough applications, if you are going to follow all the advice, if you are going to network relentlessly, and if you are going to treat getting a job like doing a full-time job then eventually you will be in the right place at the right time – and that may well appear to be luck but you will know that it isn't! We all know stories of people who appear to be catapulted into success overnight – and then we hear of the years and years of struggles they went through to achieve that success. The same principles apply in this case.

Obviously skills, experience and qualifications are a huge factor and we will address a lack of these in Chapter 3 of this book (because of course you can address these too) but for the moment I want to address the fact that people with less of those often get better jobs than people with more of those. Why is that? Well, I have seen tremendous real-life evidence that it is due to their persistence and implementation. This comes from them taking the time to understand thoroughly the tools and techniques that will secure the job – which is what I will lay out in this book. It then comes from them implementing these techniques consistently and quickly – and that comes from building and then implementing your Action Plan.

Yesterday has gone, learn from it but don't go back there

Often by the time young people come to us they are quite disillusioned because they have not been successful to date in securing a great job. They tell us the mistakes they think they have made and how it has ruined chances for them. That's when we always tell them to draw a line under it, i.e. learn from it but recognise that was then and this is now. We cannot change what has gone on before and so there is absolutely no point in dwelling on it, this will only cause negative feelings. Instead what we need to do is draw some conclusions from it, and then move on!

Family and friends peer pressure

Many of us are lucky enough to have lots of friends, family and acquaintances around us who care enough about us to give their opinions on what we should and shouldn't be doing. They may also have high expectations of our time and want us to stay the same – to not change – because they are comfortable with the version of us that they know. This can be great but sometimes it is not helpful in our quest to find our new job and build our career. The reason for this is that they are not experts in the subject of job seeking. They may think they are because of their own experiences and because they have probably found their own jobs in the past – but compared to professionals who have placed thousands of people into their first jobs, they are not experts. So explain to them that you are grateful for their advice but actually you would prefer to pursue the Action Plan you are building here. Announce the Action Plan, go through it with them, let them see how time-consuming it is going to be and let them understand how committed you are to implementing it. This will help them understand and avoid you hurting their feelings or completely alienating them.

Also it will help you manage time commitments. Finding a great job is a big job in itself. If you do it properly you will be very busy! The only way to make sure you get this done is to maintain a proper electronic diary and in it enter all the job-seeking activities that you are committed to carrying out. So for example, if you are going to work on your job search every morning then block out your diary from 9am till midday every day and treat these as business meetings. Do not accept random social invitations or stay in bed late, and manage other people's expectations by letting them know that at certain times of the day you are unavailable to them.

Self-awareness, self-management and time management

Managing your own mindset and your time is also a critical component of your job search. Contrary to popular stories that people love to tell about how unbelievably quickly they secured a job, for most of us this is a time-consuming process. It takes a huge amount of time to get our application and ourselves packaged up to make us most attractive to the employer and very often that work is done speculatively, by which I mean we do all that work with no guaranteed outcome. Preparing for and attending interviews is also hugely time-consuming and days can be 'wasted' – or so it seems. Networking events will also eat into large amounts of time but if they are in the evening one has to consider what value would otherwise have been achieved from this time. If we were only going to be watching TV or socialising for example, then surely it is better use of our time to go networking even if we may leave the event with no beneficial leads or advice on many occasions.

So – we need to prepare for this. We need to plan into our diary all the activities that are listed on our Action Plan and we need to commit to implementing them on time. The trick is to prepare our mindset to accept that this is going to be a lengthy journey and that no activity is wasted, and we must not allow ourselves to feel downhearted or disillusioned just because we do not get immediate results. Indeed each of these activities serves to improve our job search skills and techniques and because we are new at some of these, we should expect frequent failure to start with.

We also need to review our performance against this Action Plan on a weekly basis, i.e. look at what we have achieved, tick off the actions we have done and then carry forward the actions that we have not yet completed into the next week. If we have set ourselves a timeframe to secure our first job then we must catch up on any missed activities and those activities must not be hurried. If you plan for all this up front then when you are mid-way through you will be less likely to get disheartened. Self-management is similar to self-preservation: you must protect and nourish your mindset so that it stays strong for the task in hand.

The importance of looking after yourself

Protecting your mindset is one part of a much wider responsibility you have to yourself to be the most productive. It is important to look after not only your emotional wellbeing and technical know-how but also your physical and exterior being too. Firstly you will need a lot of energy to perform at your best. Energy comes from good nutrition, exercise and enough sleep. It really is quite simple: if you fuel your body with good nutrition rather than artificial junk food then you will be more energetic. The same applies if you exercise – this gets the blood flowing and makes you feel more awake than if you don't exercise, surprisingly! Sufficient sleep, which for most is eight hours a night without the distractions of late night TV, laptops and social media interruptions, will make you feel far more energetic and alert too, and you will look better. Which leads me on to the subject of personal appearance.

To achieve a good first impression you do not have to be the most attractive and best looking. However, you do need to make a good impression and there are a few simple techniques to achieve this. The first is your physical grooming. This means immaculate cleanliness of hair, nails, teeth and every other part of your body as well as all your clothes, shoes, and any bag you carry. You want to give off an image and aroma of fresh cleanliness; hair should be cut or neatly styled, heavy jewellery or make-up is unnecessary and can be off-putting. Tattoos and all piercings may need to be covered up or removed depending on the employer. There is little point in making a statement with your looks but not getting the job – especially if you have worked so hard to secure the interview.

By having all the above in place, you will naturally feel more self-confident and that will make you appear self-confident – so it is really a win–win to follow these simple guidelines. I have included a section in the Action Plan for you to write down as part of your brand a nutrition plan, an exercise plan and a grooming plan. Become the you that you want to be by producing and following this Action Plan – it is as critical a part of the plan as any other and will set you in great stead for the rest of your life, well beyond finding that first job.

So to conclude this part of the book, I am urging you to think about all aspects of your own wellbeing and personal strength, to not be afraid to be different and to not be worried about blending in with the crowd, to take control of all aspects of yourself and your time, to prepare an Action Plan and to *follow* it – i.e. to fight for your ideal career.

Chapter 3

Overcoming Personal Barriers and Beliefs – Get Rid Of Objections

One of the main things preventing young people achieving their first job is themselves – they literally get in their own way! This is because humans are excellent at telling themselves reasons why they cannot achieve things. Our subconscious voice will make up as many excuses for us as possible and it does this for self-preservation so we don't feel so bad about ourselves! What we need to do is recognise these excuses for what they are: barriers to our success. If we believe them, we will give up trying rather than addressing them and overcoming them in order to be successful. So this chapter is about identifying when this happens and how to overcome these barriers. Looking for and securing a job is about so many things other than preparing a good CV and interviewing well; we must make sure we eradicate all these personal barriers first, so let's examine them in more detail.

There are no jobs

Yes there are! At this point in time there are thousands of jobs available in the UK and that's just the ones that are advertised; this excludes all the hidden jobs I have talked about. Take two minutes to just Google the job title you are interested in and you will immediately see vacancies. There are jobs – lots of them – and actually there is a tremendous skills shortage, which means that employers are even more desperate to fill those vacancies and so might consider people who have some of the skills and then train them with the rest.

The jobs on offer are not good enough for me/don't pay enough

We all have to start somewhere and if you find that you are consistently being offered jobs that you don't want but cannot get the jobs that you do, then stop and reconsider for a moment. Sometimes the salary offered in a starting job is very low, much lower than we'd like, but think about what else you may be receiving instead of financial reward such as valuable skills and experience that will ultimately lead you to the more highly paid position. Sometimes the 'pay' is not just in money, it is in experience and knowledge. The employer/employee relationship is a two-way bargain and often when the employee cannot offer very much besides a willingness to learn and a spare pair of hands then the employer is going to consider that the sharing of skills and experience is enough to compensate for the lower salary on offer. This is not a forever position and sometimes it is very worthwhile considering taking a low-paid position just to achieve those all-important skills and experience on your CV as well as an employer reference.

I have no experience

In line with the above, I would always suggest you get some somehow even if it is with little or no pay. You can try to fit in another job that pays some money at evenings and weekends. I know this is hard to fit in and may seem unfair but really it will pay off hugely in the future once you have eliminated the 'no experience' barrier. Also do consider how much experience is actually needed – often not very much – and every little counts. One month for example is much better than none. Two is better than one and so on. Every bit of experience you can get in your desired profession or even a related profession is better than none.

Don't forget that when we are preparing your CV we will want to look over your history and see a 'story' forming, i.e. that one thing led to another and was always part of your big plan. Therefore if you cannot get experience in your chosen field then don't choose any random field – choose one that is at least distantly related so you can explain at a later date that it was always part of the plan.

I don't have the right/enough qualifications

Once again you can get some. I know this is difficult, however most things in life are if they are worth achieving. Doing difficult things and succeeding at them will motivate you to go on even further, and if things were all easy everyone would be doing them! So consider what qualifications you really need and set about putting together an Action Plan to achieve them. Firstly list what you need, in order of priority. Then investigate and then list where/ how you can earn those qualifications and how long each one will take. Find out what funding options there are to pay any fees. Then find out when you can apply to do them and whether they can be done on a distance learning or part-time course. It doesn't matter what level you have to start at – high or low – the important thing is to do something about the 'no qualifications' issue rather than settling for it as a barrier forever. Many private training providers will offer various start dates throughout the year so you don't have to wait for formal term-time starts and many will deliver these qualifications over the internet or part-time face to face. They will also tell you what funding options are available.

I have no money

This is a very real and immediate issue for many, many job seekers but it can be and often is tackled. The important first step is to identify exactly what you need as a minimum in order to carry out your job search. This must exclude any luxury items and anything whatsoever that is not critical to the job search if you are really serious about achieving that goal of a great job. Once you have identified this minimum amount then you need to consider what type of part-time work you can get to cover some of these costs even though it may not be relevant in terms of experience. It is very acceptable to have on a CV some work experience that has been done literally to tide one over while job searching. This is explained as a means to an end and so can be legitimately added to the Action Plan.

I have no connections

Firstly I would suggest you have no connections *yet* – i.e. if you follow the Action Plan then part of that will see you building up a great network that is filled with connections. Secondly though, what is a connection? People often think this has to be someone at the top of the tree able to open doors of a company and literally give you a job. However, a connection is so much more than that. Very often it is someone who knows someone who might be recruiting. For example, it might be a parent of one of your friends who works in an industry similar to the one you are targeting. It might be a teacher who knows someone who has offered work experience within a company previously or a training provider who has connections to many employers. It might be the job centre who can put you in touch with employers. It might be a friend who has secured a job in a company that you would also now like to work for and they can point you in the right direction for an interview. It might be a recruiter who has placed in a company previously although currently they have no vacancies etc., etc. So you see a connection can be second- or third-hand.

I was sitting on a park bench during the Wimbledon Half-Marathon because I had pulled a muscle and so had to sit out of the race halfway round. Sitting next to me on the bench was a lady who had just done the same thing and so we got talking. It turned out she was waiting for her husband to finish and so was I. We started talking about work and it turned out her husband worked in an industry my own son was targeting. When I mentioned this she suggested that I take his number. I did and subsequently passed it to my son who made contact with the guy on LinkedIn the following day and then they met for coffee and an informal chat a few days later. No job has come of it yet but my son is now on that radar and suddenly has a connection where he didn't before.

So hopefully you can now see that you most definitely do have many connections and that they are everywhere and you can meet them anywhere; all you need to do is keep your eyes open for them and then you can build on them. They will be at parties, on the bus, at college – literally everywhere if you look!

Having made those connections, what can you do with them? Well, you need to connect with them on LinkedIn, Twitter or Facebook (but leave out Facebook if it has personal information on there you wouldn't want an employer to see) and you then need to tell them what you are seeking and keep them updated. If they do offer advice or an introduction, take it gratefully and keep them updated on progress. Offer to help them if you ever can and therein is the secret of a great network of connections.

I'm just not good enough

I do hear this often and I always ask: "Who says? Have all employers told you this or are you telling yourself?" If you have been told it by employers or indeed by peers or so-called friends then use it as 'rocket fuel' for you to get ahead and prove them wrong! I personally find that being told I cannot do something is the absolutely best thing someone can do for me because it motivates me to do it and prove them wrong! I have numerous examples of this, but two of my favourites are these. Firstly, once I had run my business for a few years I wanted to move into a new, much larger office. The office I chose was huge in comparison to the existing one and very expensive. I started enquiries on it and set about planning it in detail. I couldn't understand why some members of my team weren't as excited about it as I was until I overheard one of them say that they would do what I asked but that we would probably still be sitting in the same office this time next year! That was enough for me! Suffice to say we were in the new office, all refurbished, six months from that date. What's more, I went on to open several more offices! Another example is this book you are holding in your hands. I am very busy and people told me I would never have the time to write a book – once again this was enough 'rocket fuel' to get the job done. This can work for you too!

If on the other hand you are saying it to yourself then please re-read this chapter and give yourself a stern talking to! All barriers can be overcome – so let's just overcome them. It won't be easy but it is most certainly possible. Also let's be very honest with ourselves; you may not be good enough *yet* that doesn't mean not good enough for ever. Also what evidence do you have to back up your claim that you are not good enough yet? Is it that you are comparing yourself to others or to the media? The media is a dangerous place for those who have had their confidence knocked because it promotes such unrealistic extremes both of success and of failure. My advice would be to not read newspapers at this stage of your job search and not to listen to the news. It is nearly all bad news and when you are trying to prepare yourself and build up your own self-esteem and confidence you only want to hear good news.

Additional needs

We find many young people have additional needs such as learning difficulties or personal difficulties including homelessness, violence at home and so on. There are a variety of sources to help you overcome these issues, no matter how daunting this seems. Everyone has their own personal battles to overcome and the most important thing is to take the first step to achieve that and the first step is to find out what organisations will help and to then contact them. You can find a list of supportive organisations on www.1stjobseries.com

PART 2
ACTION

Chapter 4

Your Mission In Life, Your Life Plan and How Your Career Fits Into That

---

Having overcome various barriers that may be holding you back, it is now time to start looking forward into the future to clarify exactly what type of job you desire prior to starting your search. As the old saying goes, if you don't know where you are heading then you are not likely to get there.

The first part of this is considering your life plan and asking yourself how you want your life to be in the future. If you can be clear on this then the next part − identifying what job would suit you − is much easier because you will have set it in context of your wider life.

There are a number of other benefits to doing this too. Success in your career can be so much easier if there is synergy between your work and your life. If the two conflict it can cause considerable issues so it's great if you can avoid that conflict from the outset. Another benefit of this approach is that if you start in the future and work backwards to the present you can clarify any deadlines for yourself, e.g. if I want to be doing xyz in five years' time then I must have xyz experience/qualifications in two years' time meaning I must enrol this year! The other great thing about this approach is that it is within your power to change and review it as many times as you wish. You can look into the future, decide how you want it, work backwards to the present again and if you are not happy with the deadlines that you end up with, then scrub that out mentally and do the exercise again until you *are* happy with it. Finally, this approach really is very motivating, particularly if you are not happy with how things have gone for you career-wise so far. Sometimes it really can feel that wrong choices were made at school/college/university and that this will always prevent you from achieving your career goals. By taking this approach though, we find it helps people look at the past in context. For example, if you are 18 years old and are disappointed with progress so far, but then you start looking into the future 20 years from now, you realise that you are about to enjoy three times the amount of time you have already had at senior school and even then you will still only be 38, not even halfway through your working life! That in turn can help motivate you to really change things and start taking the actions now to achieve the career you really want. In my job I see people change career at the ages of 40, 50 and even older. I personally started my first business at the age of 39 after having a long corporate career.

How to produce your life plan

You will need a nice quiet place to do this, away from noise and distractions and certainly somewhere where you will not be disturbed, can close your eyes, and really think. Once you are comfortable the starting point is for you to close your eyes and imagine yourself into the future using a timeframe that is comfortable for you. Generally speaking we would suggest looking 15–20 years ahead, but if that is simply too far ahead for you to even contemplate, try 10 years – certainly don't do less than five.

Having decided the timeframe, start to really look at your future self. Firstly what do you look like? What are you wearing? How fit are you? What is your speech like – how do you communicate with people? What have your mannerisms become and what first impression do you give when you meet people for the first time? Really look at yourself and decide if you like what you see. If you don't then the beauty of this approach is you can erase that vision and re-imagine it. Do it until you do like what you see – then hold that thought and write it all down. This is the you that you want to become.

Secondly look at where your future self is, i.e. where you work – describe the environment, is this an office or outside or another type of organisation? Where is it? What does it look like? How long are you there each day? Once again if you start to conjure up a picture that you don't like, erase that one and imagine one that you do like and aspire to.

Next consider where your future self lives. Is it a house or a flat? Is it far away from work or close by? What is it like inside, what does it look like from the outside? How do you feel when you are in there? How much did it cost you to buy it? Do you have a mortgage or do you rent? How long are you planning to stay there?

After that imagine who you are with, and what sort of people you surround yourself with. What are your work colleagues like? Are you the boss or do you have a boss – what is your boss like? What sort of boss and/or colleague are you? What are your friends like? How do you all socialise? Are you married or with a partner? Do you have children? What is your partner like and what do they do for work?

Next how do you travel? How do you get to and from work for example? Do you travel elsewhere as part of your work? If you drive then when did you pass your test and what do you drive? How much did it cost you? When did you buy it? Also where do you go for holidays and how often? How do you travel there? What things do you enjoy when you are on holiday?

This can all be summed up in one word: visualisation. Visualisation is an extremely powerful method for cultivating your goals; it is a bit like daydreaming and imagining but with lots of detail added until you can literally feel like you are within the role you are thinking about.

Having clarified all these goals – and this might take quite a bit of time to get to something you are happy with – start to consider the 'whys' and the 'whats' and the 'hows'. Why do you want all this? Why have you imagined things to be this way? What will achievement of all this do for you? Where will it lead you? How will it make you feel? How will it make others feel about themselves and about you?

Specifically, ask yourself how badly you want things to be like this and what sorts of sacrifices you are prepared to make in order to achieve what you have visualised. If your answer to this is in any way doubtful, you must go back to the visualisation section and draw up a less ambitious set of goals (although I would always personally suggest that young people reach for the sky!). The important thing is that you reach a point where you have envisaged a picture that you are absolutely committed to and that you are prepared to do whatever is necessary to get to. Once you have this you are then in a position to produce your Action Plan.

Step 2 – Go to your Action Plan at www.1stjobseries.com and complete the Lifeplan template.

Your time line

The Action Plan leading you to this set of goals that you have envisaged is a critical part of your thinking. What you need to do at this point is to break down the time distance into manageable chunks that you can then use to create your own personal deadlines. For example, if you have used a timeframe of 10 years, you will need to start thinking that if you need to have achieved that picture in 10 years' time what will you need to have in place in nine years' time then in eight years' time then in seven and so on back to one year's time? Once you are clear on what you need to have in place in one year's time you can start to put together deadlines of what you need to have in place by the end of each month in that current year, i.e. what do you need to have in place in 11 months, in 10 months, nine months etc. back to one month's time in order to achieve that one-year goal? Next, once you have the one-month goal you can start to look at this current month and consider what deadlines you need to meet over the next four weeks within this month – and once you know that you can then consider exactly what you have to do daily for this current week that you are in.

So there you have a blueprint for planning in detail what you need to do to achieve the life of your dreams: you have envisaged exactly how you want things to be and then you have identified all the steps you need to put in place to achieve that.

This approach can be incredibly liberating, but also very daunting. I have occasionally seen people work all this out only to find that they should be doing something very different right now! If this is the case then it is simply a matter of adjusting your timeframe outwards. For example, a young lady who works for us shared her life plan with us. She wanted to have four children running around by the time she was 30 and also wanted to have been a midwife for five years prior to that. We worked out that she needed to have already started her midwifery course to have achieved that! After this exercise she adjusted her timeframe backwards to give her a bit more time to accommodate all that she wants to do.

The important point is that a huge amount can be accomplished in a very short space of time if you plan it like this. You must not feel under pressure if you don't yet have the job of your dreams. Instead see the goal clearly, work out what you have to do to achieve that goal and then set about achieving it.

Step 3 – Go to your Action Plan at www.1stjobseries.com and complete the Timeline template.

Your tracker

The final step in this life plan is to build yourself a mechanism for keeping yourself on track. What we don't want is to build this fabulous plan and then put it away never to be seen again. This plan must become part of your everyday routine. The way to do this is firstly to put your higher-level goals – I would suggest the monthly ones – on to a revision card that you can fold up and keep in your wallet. This card should be always there – always looking at you when you open your wallet! It will be a daily reminder to you of your plan and every time you have a spare minute, e.g. sitting on a bus or having a coffee, get it out and read it. Each time you achieve one of the goals on it you can have the wonderful task of ticking that goal off. This really is incredibly motivating and before you know it you will have all your goals ticked and will have to produce a new card with the next set on.

Besides the day-to-day ticking off exercise with that card, you should book in a weekly slot in your diary to look at the bigger plan and constantly review that too to see where you are and to rate your progress against it. There is absolutely nothing wrong with amending this larger plan either. You are going to change your mind as you progress along and that is absolutely fine – but only so long as you keep your plan updated so you can continue to adhere to it.

So in conclusion, why have I suggested that you create your life plan like this? Well, it is so you can put your first job, when you get it, into perspective. The first job does not equal your last job as you will have now seen. It is a stepping-stone – but a critical one. Therefore you need to stick at it for the planned period of time before moving to your next one. It is critical for you to build up a strong history of skills and experience into your CV and to do that you need to be able to demonstrate 'stickability' i.e. that you can stick at a job for at least a year and ideally for two. This shows future employers that it is worth them investing their time in training you because it appears you will not just drop them to move to another job. Having the plan will help you achieve this stickability because it will help you see the current or first job in context. It may not be your favourite but it is a means to an end and therefore you will be more inclined to complete the position and do what you committed to do before setting out for the next move.

Step 4 – Go to your Action Plan at www.1stjobseries.com and complete the Milestones template and then write up your first card and put it in your wallet!

Chapter 5

Your Chosen Career Path – The Nicher The Better

So now you have a very clear idea of your life plan and what your life will look like in a number of years' time. Included in that is your work and you now have the beginnings of an idea of what type of work you will be doing, where and with whom. The next step is to firm up the details of that work – i.e. exactly what type of work will suit you and therefore exactly what sort of job you should be seeking.

Put yourself in a box – your niche

Firstly, the nicher the better – being put in a box is good! I often meet young people who tell me they will 'try anything' and 'don't mind what they do'. There really is a major issue with this though and I always try to dissuade them from this thought. If you tell an employer that you don't mind what you do, it's almost the same as saying you don't care what you do or don't do. It's like saying that you have not thought things through, might jump from one job to the next and, in summary, really aren't worth taking a risk on. On the other hand, if you have total clarity on what you want to do and can tell an employer specifically what you aspire to, what job you want to end up in, why the job they are offering is going to help you on that path and how keen therefore you are to secure that position, then they are much more likely to want to give you the job.

With that in mind, it really is critical for you to start making some decisions regarding specifically what you want to do. Please don't worry because no one is saying that you cannot change this at a later date. The point is you need to decide on a path to at least get you part way to the future you have envisaged for yourself and so you need to choose one of those paths right now.

A method that really works is to put down all the criteria that you would be seeking in any job. Your life plan work would have helped you with this. The criteria might include things such as working with many people or working alone, working in an office or working outside, sitting at a desk or not, speaking on the telephone or not, working with your hands or not, working with certain types of people vs others, a minimum amount of money you can earn, location, travel etc., etc. Write down as many criteria you can list as possible at this stage; it doesn't matter if some are more important than others, just make sure you write down at least 10 and then reorder them in order of importance to you once you have listed them all.

Next list all the jobs you can possibly think of and also all the types of companies you can think of. You can do this by looking at job boards or on recruitment agency websites where jobs are advertised if you are really stuck. Put as many different jobs down as you can – I would suggest a minimum of 50, which will be tough but certainly do-able.

Next start to rate the jobs using the 10 criteria you have specified. Give each job one point for every criteria it fulfils; this means that each job or company can score a minimum of zero and a maximum of 10 and anything in between because you can allocate parts of a point too.

Once you have completed this exercise look at the jobs that have the highest score. Keep the top five and remove all the rest. You need to focus on your top five. Then within that top five prioritise. You then need to focus on your number 1. Eliminate numbers 3, 4 and 5. Keep number 2 up your sleeve. Now we are going for number 1 — that is your niche!

Step 5 — Go to your Action Plan at www.1stjobseries.com and complete the Niche template.

The importance of your story

In order to launch your career you set about building a story. As I have said before, an employer is keen to not only put you into a box in their mind but also wants to see that you have been aiming for the sort of job they are offering for some time and haven't just stumbled over the opportunity and decided to go for it just because it is there. This takes us back to the employer's wants and desires and their concerns. They do not want to spend time and money on someone who is going to leave them the minute a better or more suitable opportunity comes along, and you can therefore put their mind at rest in this area by having your story. Your story will consist of all the things you have done that have positioned you for this type of role and will demonstrate that you have aimed for a role such as this for some time — even if you haven't!

So your story will consist of a clear statement of what you want to achieve in your career, what qualifications and work experience you have achieved so far to help you on that path and why you think this job is totally suitable for you as part of that path. To achieve this you need to look at your past with new eyes and ask yourself how does what you have done so far fit in with what you want to do next — no matter how tenuously. It looks so much better to an employer if you can demonstrate that actually the reason you did various qualifications and courses and took various jobs was all to build up expertise to bring you to the current point. And don't think that I am encouraging you to falsify information in any way, try looking at your past first and see if you can see those links. You will be amazed at how you can find them and that your subconscious actually tends to help you make choices that do in fact lead you to a career path you will be happy in.

To illustrate this I will use Annabel as an example. Annabel wanted to study Geography at university but missed out on her place as she did not get the grade she needed in one of her A levels. Consequently she had to go through the UCAS clearing system to secure her university place and ended up studying Ergonomics. She chose this from a series of clearing options and it was most certainly not her first choice. However, it turned out that she enjoyed it and not only that but she absolutely loved the Human Factors aspect of it. In addition, she worked for me as an intern during the summer holidays and part of that work was on an HR system. Once again she didn't plan this but nevertheless she enjoyed it and learned a lot. When it came to selecting a career path she sat down to create her story. It was quite easy to pull this together into one that is very fitting for an introduction to a career in HR. She was able to take all the diverse aspects of what she had done and pull them together into a very solid story of how and why she was now interested in HR. Firstly she chose her university and that was on the basis of her sporty nature and love of socialising. Next, she chose Ergonomics out of a liking for design and communication. Thirdly she ended up working on our HR system of all things due to her interest in developing processes and procedures to achieve maximum human efficiencies. When you start consolidating all this you very soon come up with links relating to human resource and human capital. She is now consolidating this by actually doing a Masters in HR and once she has accomplished that she will be well on the way to securing a position in her chosen niche.

This can be done in the huge majority of cases because you will naturally see that there are links between the steps you have taken so far and the steps you want to take next. By doing this you can reconstruct your CV to really demonstrate that you are already more prepared than others for the role you want.

Step 6 – Go to your Action Plan at www.1stjobseries.com and complete the Your story template.

The danger of job-hopping

Your story will be more and more difficult to construct if you 'job-hop' unless of course you have been working consistently for a recruitment agency and have purposely positioned yourself as a professional temp to achieve maximum experience in a certain field. Unless that is the case though, jumping from job to job – anything with less than a year per job – really does not look good. This is further damaging if you were committed to completing a course of learning while with the employer, such as an apprenticeship. For example, if you were doing a one-year apprenticeship but only stayed there for six months before moving on, you will have a very hard time explaining to an employer how that happened. They will wonder were you pushed, in which case why or did you leave, in which case maybe you are unreliable. They may not believe you if you blame the employer as they may tend to see it from the perspective of the employer – and what's more they may well insist on taking a reference from that employer. For this reason (and others) it is very important that you honour employment commitments and that the jobs you do take have some form of link to each other.

Portfolio careers

While on the subject of selecting a career niche for yourself, I want to discuss the concept of portfolio careers. What we mean by this is that an individual will most probably have a number of (portfolio of) careers throughout their career span. This is very different from job-hopping because it is a considered career change. The first is very unlikely to be the last and it is very usual for someone who works until they are 65 to have had five different careers at least – one every decade sometimes. The obvious reason for this is that people's selection criteria for careers differ as they move through different stages of life where things like working hours, mobility and location can become more or less important as time progresses. For this reason, please do not concern yourself too much with whether or not you have applied the 'correct' criteria or come up with the 'correct' niche. The most important thing is that you have been through the process and what you have emerged with is absolutely the best choice for you right now. There is no right or wrong answer. You just need to choose a path and then follow it resolutely and make the very best of it until you come to your next crossroads, which is likely to come at a stage later in your life.

The other point to make here is that sometimes people really cannot distinguish between their top couple of choices – they truly want to pursue both because they do not want to abandon one of them. Alternatively they may already be making some money at one and cannot afford to let that go while they pursue their true ambition fully. If this is the case with you then I would suggest you really consider things very carefully. It is hard enough building up skills and experience in one field let alone two. Also consider it in hours. If you decide to take two part-time jobs in two different fields for example, you are halving the time you have to become expert in your field. Your competition will be spending *all* their time on their field and will therefore quickly zoom ahead of you. If this doesn't bother you then absolutely fine; work out your life plan accordingly and take a path that includes two niches – but this is extremely difficult and I would strongly advise against it if you can possibly avoid it.

Being unique

Finally, a word about the importance of your niche fitting who you are as a person and making sure that you use all your uniqueness as an asset and an advantage rather than conforming too much or trying to be like others or how you think you are expected to be.

Firstly your hobbies – what are they and what do they say about you, why do you like them? How do they link to your chosen niche, your ideal career and job? To answer that, think about what you do as part of your hobbies and what you know and what you feel confident doing; now try to link those qualities to the job you are seeking. Is there a link? There nearly always is – for example: "I like playing football; I want to be in sales. Football is competitive and results driven, as is sales. I believe my competitive spirit in football will underpin my ability to be competitive and results driven in sales."

Secondly your personality – emphasise it and don't change it. Once again, how does it link to the skills and qualities required for the job? For example: "I am a quiet and studious person. I enjoy detail. I want to be in accounts. Accounts requires an eye for detail, long periods of concentration and the ability to focus. I believe my quiet and studious nature will underpin my ability to be accurate and reliable within an accounts role."

Thirdly your skills – once again never waste what you have. Sometimes I see a young person considering a complete change of career very early on because they cannot get their current career off the ground. I always advise against this. If you have completed studies in a certain sector, then gained some work experience in that sector, no matter how little, you are *miles* ahead of your competition in that sector even if it doesn't yet feel like it. It would therefore be crazy to change tack and try to get into a completely different industry – unless of course you can identify clear links between your skills and experience to date and your new industry (your story). Always try to make your next move a stepping-stone building upon the skills you already have; never discard all your experience and start completely over. Even with portfolio careers there is always a link from one to the next.

So in conclusion, your uniqueness is just that – unique – and therefore an employer will want it. You have a set of skills, personal qualities and knowledge that no one else has and the more you emphasise this, the more valuable it will make you appear to an employer. Of course you need to make sure that there is a match between your qualities and the job you are seeking. It would be hard to justify being quiet and studious with wanting to be in a front line sales role. That would not be quite so believable as the examples I have cited above.

Step 7 – Go to your Action Plan at www.1stjobseries.com and complete the Your Unique Selling Points template.

Chapter 6

You're Ready –
The Marketing Plan

You are selling and the employer is buying

So now you are clear on your target, why you want to achieve that target, where it fits into your overall life plan and you have overcome any personal barriers and objections or at least have a plan and mechanism to do so. You are now ready to sell yourself to an employer and the best way to do that is to consider yourself as a product.

If you are selling to a buyer there are four main components that need to be in place: the product itself and its packaging; the potential buyers or the audience; the visibility and accessibility of the product to them; and then the sales process itself including the after sales and support.

If you think of yourself as a product you must take into account that you are always going to be a product in development. Like an Apple iPhone, there will be constant new versions of you! You must be clear on not only what you can offer *now* but also what you have the potential to offer in the future. Also just like a product you must be packaged up as attractively as possible. If you think about the iPhone again it comes in an immaculate packaging, very sleek and attractive. It also comes with guarantees and after sales service and support. Also it is highly visible – you can go and find one to buy very easily. We need to address all components of your packaging in this way too.

Let's take each of these components separately.

The Product and Packaging – the CV and letter

The first thing that is often seen of you by the buyer is your CV and maybe a covering letter. This is your advertisement, your marketing tool – and it has to be convincing and leaving the buyer wanting to know more otherwise it will go in the bin. This is where your story comes in which I described earlier. If you think about the buyer and what's in their mind, it is quite simple. They need someone to fill a gap they have identified and this will always be related to them wanting to get more business through the door or to save money somehow. All roles ultimately relate to one of these two aims. What they don't want is someone who is going to lose them business or cause them to waste money and they will usually be very nervous about that and avoid anyone who even hints at that. Danger signs for an employer include short stays at employers (could indicate lack of performance), gaps in the CV (could indicate lack of ambition and drive) and huge diversity (could indicate lack of direction). Good signs for an employer include a year or more with an employer or at least a clear indication that a shorter period was always planned from the outset, no gaps in the chronology of the CV, and links between each step.

Basically the buyer needs to be able to read the CV – understand easily what you have done so far, where you have been and what you are aiming to do in the future. This needs to be believable and convincing, clear with no suspicious gaps or unanswered questions to cause doubts in the buyer's mind. Although it is a marketing tool, it must not contain every superlative you can think of to describe yourself; things like 'hard-working' should go without saying. Instead what should be there is hard evidence of things you have done to back up that statement. You need to position yourself as a solution provider rather than a problem to be dealt with – and you need to make clear what your major achievements are and ensure they are relevant to the reader. For example, if your CV is going to an accountant who wants you to work diligently checking ledgers, a major achievement of jumping out of an aeroplane will be less relevant than to an employer who wants bold and brave new sales people. So your CV must be relevant to the reader. This is where your story comes in – the story that I have mentioned previously – and it is why you must do the thinking about your niche before you finalise your CV.

Step 8 – Go to your Action Plan at www.1stjobseries.com and complete the CV template.

The Product and Packaging – your elevator pitch

An elevator pitch is a one-minute speech that you can deliver about yourself any time you are asked what you do or what you want to do in your career. It is called an elevator pitch because it is based on the idea that if you were caught in an elevator (lift) with someone who could hire you and they asked you what you want to do, you would only have the time while in the lift to describe it! An elevator pitch must convey in as few words as possible what you want, and why an employer would be lucky to have you. There is a template in the Tools section of this book and online, and once you have written up your elevator pitch you should rehearse it in front of the mirror until you are word perfect and can just reel it off whenever you feel like it with no nerves or hesitation.

Step 9 – Go to your Action Plan at www.1stjobseries.com and complete the Elevator Pitch template.

The Product and Packaging – LinkedIn profile

The next part of your packaging is your LinkedIn profile. If you don't already have one, now is the time to set one up on https://www.linkedin.com. If you do then you must review it in accordance with the following. For any of you not familiar with it, LinkedIn is the business users' Facebook – it has over 13 million users in the UK alone and over 300 million users worldwide. It contains all levels of workers from every type of business you can imagine and every country. It is a massive advertising window for you because it is often the first port of call for recruiters – both agency recruiters as well as recruiters looking for new staff for their own company. Jobs are advertised there and also you can be found on there if someone is searching for someone with your skills. Therefore you need to ensure that this 'window to the business world' looks like you want it to before anyone sees it! The LinkedIn profile must contain the same details as your CV – they must match. It is best to produce your CV first and then complete your LinkedIn profile. The great thing about this is that you can update it very easily whenever you want and as many times as you want. It is very important to have a businesslike headshot on there – no headshot is an absolute no no – and a social one, one where you are clearly out at a social event, maybe with someone's arm around you or where you are not wearing business attire is also not recommended at all. You need to be wearing business attire and have a simple headshot – look up mine to get the idea and connect with me if you want to.

There is more to do with your LinkedIn profile once you have set it up but more on that later. Let's first move to the next component of your packaging – your Facebook and Twitter accounts.

The Product and Packaging – Facebook and Twitter

I would suggest that even Facebook has a role in your job search, despite the fact that it is probably all about your social life and your connections are all family and friends. I know that Facebook goes in and out of fashion and that many young people have moved across to Twitter and Instagram, however, Facebook might still have a part to play in your packaging. The first point to be clear on though is that you absolutely must ensure that your Facebook is locked. I have on more than one occasion not appointed a candidate because I have seen things on their Facebook that don't reflect the sort of person I need to hire. You must keep it on lock down and review this regularly because Facebook frequently alter settings. However, within your Facebook network where you no doubt have hundreds if not thousands of connections, you have a wonderful opportunity to reach out to see if anyone can point you in the right direction. This is your current *network* so *use it*! A simple status saying: "I am looking for my first job in xyz, does anyone know anyone at all who works in this area who they can introduce me to – inbox me if so," might just obtain a critical contact for you. You will be amazed how many of your contacts' friends, parents, siblings etc. work in your chosen niche! Don't only do this once – keep re-posting it until you get some responses and then keep them up-to-date with your search. People might take the mickey out of you initially but after a while you will find them so supportive of you, and when you finally announce you have found your first job you will be amazed how many likes you get!

With regard to Twitter, the same applies. I am going to advise you in Chapter 6 on how to start following important people within your chosen industry. Once you follow them they might look at you. What will they see? If it's not in line with your professional image then keep your existing one for personal use and lock down your settings and set up another more professional one with your professional headshot. I will tell you how to start using this when we get into the Sales Process section.

Step 10 – Set up or amend your LinkedIn, Twitter and Facebook profiles.

The Product and Packaging – your email address

Your email address might be quite old and you might even have the year of your birth in it, which is common for Hotmail users. Unfortunately you might also have an email address that was amusing when you were younger but now doesn't quite convey the professional image you want it to! For example, drunkenlad93@hotmail.com is not quite the email address you want an employer to be writing to! I would suggest that in any event you get yourself a new one sharpish and I would always suggest you obtain firstname@firstnamelastname.com or .co.uk. For example, I have an email address which is: angela@angelamiddleton.com. This is extremely easy for anyone to remember and looks very professional. It also allows me to have my own domain which is useful for my own use later on if I want a personal website separate from my business website. If you go online and Google domains there are many sites where you can purchase your own domain and then have your email address set up. This will probably cost you somewhere in the region of £25 a year, but it is really worth it and will stand you in good stead for the rest of your professional life.

Once you have the email address set up then you need to standardise your signature. You can set this up so that every email you send contains a standard section at the end containing your details. Into that you can put your telephone number, a photo of you, a link to your LinkedIn and Twitter profiles, any statements about you, maybe even a link to your CV or to a video about you. I will talk more about videos and photos in CVs in section 3.

Step 11 – Purchase your new domain and set up your new email address.

The Product and Packaging – your phone number and voicemail

Remember to personalise your voicemail and to listen to it! I know that young people often prefer to interact via social media and 'talking' can actually mean conversing on WhatsApp, for example. However, if a prospective employer or recruitment agent wants to get hold of you they will often do so by leaving you a voicemail. It is therefore imperative that you listen to your voicemails the minute they come up. It really does not look good if an unemployed person who appears to have no commitments says that they did not call back earlier because either they didn't listen to the message or they were too busy. This can be extremely off-putting for the employer and could lose you the job opportunity right away before you are even at the interview stage.

Your voicemail should typically say something like: "Hello, you have reached the voicemail of Angela Middleton, I am sorry I can't take your call right now, however please leave a message and I will call you back as soon as possible."

Step 12 – Re-record your voicemail message and ensure notifications for voicemails are switched on!

The Product and Packaging – your business cards

You probably don't have business cards at this stage but now is a very good time to get them. I bought my son some when he was 18 and he wondered why but a year later he was using them at networking events and interviews. My recommendation is that you keep them very simple and plain, with a small professional photo on them if you wish (although this will date them), and just your full name, email address and mobile number. I would put your town and city but not your full address. I would also give yourself a title relating to your job search, e.g. Analyst if you want to be an analyst and so on. It's amazing that once you start calling yourself something, other people will too and you will hear recruiters saying to each other: "I have this analyst on our books... etc." just because that is the title on the CV or business card! You can order business cards on the internet for very little cost or even free – just google 'free business cards' and many sites will come up offering you your first set of cards for free.

Step 13 – Order your new business cards.

The Product and Packaging – your brand

Your brand is a less tangible thing about you that is nevertheless hugely important. What do we mean by your brand? Well if you think about David Beckham, what do you think? People say things like tattoos, football, winning, success, family, voice, Victoria, etc. – his brand is all of these things. These are the things that make him admirable and different.

So consider yourself and what people think and say about you and then consider what you *want* them to think and say about you and then you can start to cultivate the brand you want.

Firstly your values – you need to think about what they are and be clear what they are, i.e. what is important to you and on what basis do you want people to admire you. Do you want to be admired for your looks, for your knowledge, for the way you speak, the way you dress, the long hours you work, the short hours you work? This all boils down to your own values and what you think is admirable. Once you are clear on this you can start to really enhance that brand and become the most admirable version of yourself possible.

So this comes down to visualisation again – think about someone you really admire and would like to be. Then think about why that is – what is it about them that you admire? When you have an answer to that then you will be able to document your values and know what it is you want people to think and say about you. This is your brand.

For example, let's say you really admire Alan Sugar. Why do you admire him? It could be because of the money he has or it could be because of the power he has. It could be because of his poor background and how he has had to work so hard to achieve what he has. Maybe it's because of his TV stardom or his help in Government.

Let's say you admire him because of how hard he has worked to get there. This means you value hard work. Therefore you want to portray hard work. Therefore how can you do that? You can document all the hours you work – talk about it in the CV and the interview etc. Don't forget though that not everyone will value things the same as you – but broadly speaking when in an employment interview situation it is likely that they do.

Brand experts actually say there are 12 types of brands that we humans aspire to as shown in this diagram and that once you decide on a brand that best suits you, you can really cultivate everything about you to suit this category.

The Product and Packaging – your appearance

What image do you want to cultivate and project? If you want to work in a corporate environment, pick an image of someone who you think looks very corporate and who fits right in. Then question that image: what is it about that person that makes them fit in? Is it what they are wearing, how they are standing, their facial expression, their hair etc.? Then when you have decided on that, you can copy it! There is a lot to be said for copying people whom you admire and then over time you will find you become more and more like them! Obviously, if you are not impressed by a corporate image for example, you need to question why you are considering a job in that area; the sort of job you are aiming to achieve needs to be in line with the brand and image you admire. If you admire a more arty image for example, then it would probably be more comfortable for you to be seeking a role where people dress like that. Take a look at workers in the City of London and compare them to the workers walking around Soho for example; you will see financial people vs. media people and this will illustrate my point.

You may not think it but these are indeed tools and templates for you to use that will increase your chances. Whether we like it or not, research says that more than 90% of our decision-making is based on what we see and not what we hear. Therefore how we look and behave and appear is hugely important in order to be hired. Personal branding is a concept used more and more in business and it is not just about what we are wearing but how we are wearing it, how we speak, how we are groomed and our mannerisms. There are some ways to play this all safe and I would suggest that you implement these basics, and then on top of that if you want to look slightly more edgy, you can go ahead and add to it. The basics are as follows:

For women: Blow-dried and shiny hair, neat short painted nails, opaque or clear tights (not patterned), skirt to just above the knee or just below or tailored trousers, suit jacket, blouse, scarf, necklace, plain medium-heeled shoes, any tattoos covered, medium to light make-up, light perfume, light earrings, no other visible piercings.

For men: smart, clean and shiny hair, neatly cut and styled, if you have long hair then tie it back and if you have a beard make sure it is neatly trimmed and tidy, short clean nails, dark suit with white shirt and plain tie with a small knot, dark socks and polished shoes with no buckles etc., no jewellery, no visible tattoos or piercings at all, not even ear piercings.

Both should carry a briefcase containing a smart notebook and smart pen. Mobile phone should be switched off, not silent. Coat if appropriate should be dark and held over arm when walking into the interview and left on back of chair or handed to assistant if they ask.

None of the above might fit in with your style, however we are talking tools and techniques here. These are the tried and tested ways of enabling you to pass your interview. If it is necessary for you to project an image which maybe is not familiar to you then I would advise that you try it. We want to maximise your chances of passing an interview and the above will do that for you!

The Product and Packaging – your voice

Your voice is another really powerful and influential aspect of your brand. Generally speaking, clearer, louder voices convey more confidence than muffled and quiet voices. So you must practise speaking more clearly and at a louder volume. Also if your voice tends to go high when you are nervous then try to take the pitch down a little. It may sound funny but read out paragraphs to yourself and record them on the phone. Do this with your normal voice and then with a slightly louder, deeper, clearer voice. You will be able to see for yourself which one sounds more confident and it is the more confident voice that you should cultivate to use in any employment situation, either when you are seeking your first job or when you are within it. Another good tip is to speak out loud in front of a mirror or get someone to watch you and give you feedback. Tell them to be hard on you!

The Product and Packaging – your mannerisms

Mannerisms are things you do without really thinking but they convey so much and if you can control them it will really help you to project a confident image. If you film yourself having a conversation with someone for 10 minutes you will really see what I mean here. Mannerisms mainly relate to body language but can also relate to things that you say and the way you say them too. Various common mannerisms to avoid are: folding arms, slouching in a chair, tapping a foot or a pen, yawning openly, scratching or picking or nail biting, speaking with eyes closed or looking away when speaking, coughing or sneezing without a tissue, slurping drinks, chewing etc.

Mannerisms to develop include: sitting up straight, giving great eye contact, folding hands in lap so as not to use them too much, folding ankles, smiling, not interrupting, listening well, being enthusiastic. All of these will put the other person at ease too and they will enjoy speaking to you more.

Again, if you have a good friend you trust then get them to tell you what your mannerisms are that you need to stop during an interview, e.g. fiddling with your hair or jewellery, saying certain phrases (I know someone who says 'like' all the time – it drives me mad!). Get your friends to be really hard on you!

The Product and Packaging – your habits

Habits are things that you do and include: the time you get up, the food you eat, the amount of exercise you do, how often you socialise, who you socialise with and how you socialise, how you spend your weekends – generally how you organise yourself. We all have the choice of cultivating habits that will make us more successful and enhance our brand. According to research, repetition of behaviours for three weeks is enough to cultivate a habit. Positive habits that will always impress an employer include: being early into work, eating well and not at your desk, exercising, socialising in a way that gives you something useful to talk about rather than just going to the pub for example, always preparing a "things to do" list for the next day and so on. Habits will convey a lot and can be the difference between someone describing you as organised and disciplined vs. disorganised.

The Product and Packaging – your knowledge of trends

Whatever your niche, there will be trends within it that you should make yourself aware of and keep up-to-date on. For example, if you want to work in investment banking there will be key events happening in the industry and there will be main players – both companies and individuals – that are being written about in the industry press. You can find all this out via Google. Finding the largest companies within the industry you have selected will enable you to know where to start. Once you know who they are, you can Google them to see what is the latest being said about them. You can also look at the most senior people who work for them and see what's being said about them. This way you will be able to find out the general themes and events that they are all aware of. You can also follow individuals and companies on Twitter, which can give you a day-by-day account of key events. All of these things will really help you become knowledgeable about your chosen niche and this in turn will enhance your brand as a budding professional.

The Product and Packaging – testimonials and sponsors/mentors

You can do so much to enhance your own brand, as I have described above, but to have other people say great things about you too does wonders with building your reputation. You can start this by gathering testimonials from absolutely everyone you can think of who might be relevant and there should be a theme to these. For example, if you want to present a very hard-working image then you will want to have as many testimonials as possible saying how hard-working you were and in what context. Testimonials are like references but are shorter and less formal; usually they are just a couple of sentences in a quote that say things like: "John worked as a weekend shop assistant for me and during that time I was extremely impressed with how hard he worked and how reliable he was – I would highly recommend him." Something like this when said in similar ways by a few people and then presented all together in one place can have a remarkable impact. Therefore do consider absolutely everyone you know who could give you a testimonial and ask them for a quote! This can range from your school teachers, any current tutors, recruitment agents that you have got to know, managers of any organisations where you have offered voluntary help, obviously managers in any jobs you have had, no matter if they were just job experience. In this way most people are able to obtain a handful of testimonials at least.

The other real support to your brand would be a sponsor/ mentor. A sponsor/mentor is really a connection – someone who will go round talking about you in glowing terms wherever and whenever they get a chance. Sometimes this can be a teacher, or it can be a boss, or it can be a friend or a friend's parent or even one of your own family members – anyone who has agreed to advise you and support you and really wants you to do well and who circulates with others who might be able to refer you to suitable opportunities.

Step 14 – Go to your Action Plan at www.1stjobseries.com and complete the Personal Brand template – here you can find an image you most admire, analyse it to see why you admire it, copy it, make sure that the image you like fits in with the role you are aiming for, and if not then revise the role you are seeking.

The Audience

Now that you have your packaged product ready for sale and it looks as attractive as it can possibly be, it is time to identify the best audience for that product. This is where you will be identifying which employers are most likely to want that product, which is you, and also how they will want to access and identify it. What you want to end up with here is as large a database as possible of potential people you can contact about your job search. This must not be any random list though, it must contain only those individuals who will have an interest or can help you and also you will want in that list their contact details including their social media addresses, email addresses, postal addresses, locations and job titles if appropriate. I would aim for 1,000 names. This is generally a pretty easy target to achieve once you put your mind to it.

The Audience - top businesses

You can start by identifying the top 100 businesses that you would like to work for, taking into account your preferences on niche, their location, how many people they employ, whether they are advertising jobs on their website. This is usually the quickest part of the task and can generally be done on Google.

The Audience - top people

Next you need to identify the top 500 'movers and shakers' in your chosen industry – these are top-level managers in the industry. You will tend to find these by searching each of the company names from your list, first from LinkedIn and then from Twitter and from

Google. By doing this you should be able to identify five names of managers at each of your preferred companies. By using this method, you should also be able to find out their email addresses, postal addresses, job titles, phone numbers, locations – and if they use Twitter and update LinkedIn, even their views!

The Audience – experts

Next you need to identify experts within your chosen industry and to do this you generally need to establish what the associations and memberships are that these companies and people belong to. So, for example, if I Google 'Associations for Recruitment in UK', up will come APSCO (Association of Professional Staffing Companies) and REC (the Recruitment and Employment Confederation). Both of these have membership lists (usually the members are companies) and it is these members that you next want on your list. I could then, for example click into the REC website and on there is a members list. I can put in a postcode and up will pop all the recruiter members in that postcode. This is a wonderful way for you to find more companies and influencers in your chosen sector. You can then go through that list and add another 100 companies to the list of businesses above and then you can go and do stage two again to obtain five more names and details of people within each of those companies.

You should also add all the contacts of the individuals who actually run the associations. They will know who all the members are and may well be able to introduce you to any that are recruiting. This is actually a potentially massive opportunity because not only do they know all their members but they are keen to add value to their members, so if they can do that by introducing great new talent to those members (like you!), they will do that because it makes them look good!

Also you can look at recent events that have taken place within your industry, conferences etc. These will usually identify people who have spoken at the conference as well as companies that have had stands there and individuals that have organised the whole thing. All of these companies and individuals should go on your list too. For every company you find you should try to find five people from that company to go on your list.

The Audience – recruitment agencies

Any recruiters within your industry should go on your list. I have just described how you could identify recruiters in your sector via the REC website. I just put London into their search button and it identified over 10,000 recruiters. It is a good idea therefore for you to click on a sector, which will narrow the search down a bit. You can then identify all the recruitment companies that specialise in your sector and then you can go on to LinkedIn, Google, Twitter to obtain the details of their main consultants – and these should all go on to your list as they will know about hidden jobs that are not advertised.

The Audience – colleagues and friends

This is a very important set of people that must go on your list. I know that people often don't like to ask favours but think of it more that all you are doing is letting them know what you are looking for and asking them if they know anyone who might be interested in hiring and that they can pass your details to. You are not asking this set of people for a job, you will instead be asking them to give you introductions to others who may be in a position to do so.

The Audience – school/college/training provider

They will all have connections with employers too and all of them are now targeted to maintain a record of their leavers and how they have progressed. Therefore they will be only too pleased to hear from you about your progress and your job search and in return you can ask them if they can introduce you to anyone who may be able to help you.

The Audience – industry events

There are always industry events going on within every industry – they are generally advertised on things like www.Eventbrite.com and often they are free! Attending an event such as this can be quite nerve-wracking if you are not used to it; however, armed with your new image and your business cards you should most certainly try it. Successful networking is a huge subject actually, but in the next section I will provide an overview of how to make this work for you in your job search. At the very least you would want to attend and collect an attendee list from them (they usually produce one) because that will enable you to add more names to your list of people who are very active in the industry right now.

Step 15 – Go to your Action Plan at www.1stjobseries.com and compile your target list in the Audience template.

How to Make Yourself Visible to The Audience – The Sales Process

So now we have the product and we have identified the buyer! We now need to match the two together and this is the sales process. So often, job seekers launch straight into this part of the process not having covered any of the ground that I have mentioned above, and are then surprised when they send application after application without success. I hope now you have an understanding of the sort of preparation that can take place to maximise your chances, you can see why that is. If you don't prepare, you are not giving yourself the best chance. Whether it's revising for an exam, whether it's dressing up for a party where you hope to meet a new partner or whether it's preparing to find a new job, preparation is key and really is worth the time. It can save you so much time later on and get you the result you want so much more quickly, which really will boost your confidence! Now that you are prepared we can move on to the sales process and actually contacting and talking to the employers.

The Touch Points in The Sales Process

Firstly we need to understand that sales processes can take a variable length of time to be successful. Research says the average length of time to sell something is less relevant than the average number of 'touch points'. Touch points are the number of times you 'touch' or in other words make contact with the buyer. The research varies but what it does say is that the average number of times is 16! That means on average you need to make contact 16 times before getting success and don't forget that this is an average, meaning often it will take more than that. No wonder therefore that so many times I hear from youngsters that they have had no success in their job search despite sending out many, many applications. One of their issues is that they have only made a single touch point with each buyer – nowhere near enough according to the research! And so we see that the time taken to achieve success in job hunting is less about elapsed time of search in terms of days and weeks and months, it's more about the number of times we approach the same companies. This is a critically important point for you to understand before starting the sales process.

Having understood this point, it is necessary to plan the number and type of touch points that you will undertake for each target buyer. Broadly speaking those touch points will include:

1. Face-to-face at networking events

2. E-shots

3. Letters

4. Phone calls

5. Job applications for specific jobs

6. Twitter approaches (retweets etc.)

7. LinkedIn approaches (connections, likes etc.)

8. Volunteering

9. Referral from someone who works there

10. Personal visits

There are more but these are the main ones and, as you will see, 10 are listed here. Thus if you aim to do each of these twice, at least then you are aiming for at least above the average that research says will achieve success. Let's talk about each of these in turn.

The Sales Process – face-to-face at networking events

This is probably the most daunting method so I will address it first. All the rest are easy after this one has been mastered! The benefits of attending these are so significant that it really is a highly recommended activity. Benefits include being seen – you really must be seen and start having your face recognised by at least a few people in the industry. Another benefit is it gives you practice at delivering your elevator pitch and also an opportunity to discover the sort of questions people will ask you and to practise how you might respond to them. Thirdly it will pull you out of your comfort zone which in itself is a good thing because by doing that you will expand your comfort zone. Fourthly it is an unusual and brave thing to do – most people will be impressed to find that you are doing this off your own bat and that you are so proactive in getting your career off the ground. It will make you appear as a self-starter (which you are) and employers always value that.

Generally speaking, you can Google up events that relate to your chosen industry and find that they are taking place everywhere and anywhere. Other places to find out about events are the company websites, Twitter and LinkedIn where tons of events are advertised. There will be conferences, awards, networking events, speeches, industry exhibitions etc. and very often these will be free. The task here is firstly to identify when and where they will be happening and how you can gain access. Then book them all into your diary and make sure you keep them as appointments that must be kept rather than nice to dos. Because these are daunting it will be very easy for you to decide not to attend them so you must make a commitment to yourself that you will keep them.

When the day arrives, dress appropriately as if for an interview. Take several copies of your CV in a nice smart plastic wallet together with a box of your business cards. Rehearse your elevator pitch in front of the mirror so that you are ready to deliver it as soon as anyone asks you about yourself – and then set off in plenty of time to be early. It is much more daunting to be last in when everyone else is already talking than it is to be one of the first, when you can make yourself known to the organisers, request a list of attendees and anything else that is available such as an agenda. You will find the organisers themselves will be impressed if you tell them you are there to network as you are seeking your first career opportunity and they will be more than willing to accept your card, and of course you should take theirs. The aim of attending the event is threefold:

1. To learn more about the industry and who operates within it (i.e. what companies and what people).

2. To meet as many of those people as possible and to collect their cards.

3. To obtain as many referrals as possible and to be seen.

4. To connect with all the attendees afterwards to add to your list.

The most proven method of this working that I have seen is to firstly introduce yourself in a friendly way to the organisers that you see – as many of them as you can. Start with: "Hi, I'm (your name), I am here to find out more about the industry and to meet people who might be able to help me start my career in it. Who would you suggest I talk to in particular today?" They will give you some advice. Once they have, then thank them very much and ask for their card. Usually they will give you one and when they do, say: "Thank you very much and here's mine – if you know of anyone who might be looking for a hard-working junior entrant to their business." Then a friendly handshake and smile and move on.

Next you want to talk to the people mentioned. If you haven't had a chance to speak to the organiser then just decide on your own list – and if there is no list and you really have no idea who to talk to (this is not recommended and probably not likely if you have done your research) then just approach people who are on their own or in twos rather than groups as this is easier. For these, just walk up and say: "Hello, do you mind if I join you for a minute?" They will say: "Of course, do please join us." Then say similar as before: "Hi, I'm (your name), I am here to find out more about the industry and to meet people who might be able to help me start my career in it – what do you do?" They will tell you and then you can say: "That's really interesting, it would be great to get your advice on how I can make a start in this industry – what would you advise?" They'll give you some advice and once they have, then thank them very much and ask for their card. Again, usually they will give you one and when they do, say: "Thank you very much and here's mine – if you know of anyone who might be looking for a hard-working junior entrant to their business." Then a friendly handshake and smile and move on. Sometimes you might be really lucky and they'll tell you they are looking for someone themselves! Other times they will tell you specifically who to contact besides themselves – make sure you write this down!

Very important: before you move on to speaking to the next person, look at the card(s) or numbers you have been given and write on the back a few words so you remember who the person was and what they do – things like 'dark hair, tall, accountant, been there six years'.

The above takes a lot of courage and nerve but it will impress people and so it is well worth you putting in the effort with it. It is also tiring so if there is an all-day event you will want to take a break at lunchtime before starting the afternoon session, and if there is a choice I would always suggest doing the morning session instead of the afternoon because that way you can speak to the organisers as I have mentioned above.

Once you have obtained all your cards and had lots of meetings, it is essential you get home and write it all up. You may think you will remember everyone tomorrow but trust me, you won't; you will mix people up, forget what they said and this will lose you opportunities.

Another thing to be very cautious about: do not take the easy route and just hand out all your cards to everyone. If you return from one of these events and have collected no cards, you will have nothing to follow up – you won't remember who you have met and you won't be able to add them to your list.

Regarding what to do with all the cards – well, you must do something and quick! Firstly connect with them on LinkedIn that same day if possible when you are fresh in their mind (don't forget they will have met lots of people too) saying: "Dear (their name), it was great to meet you today at (the event). Thank you very much for your advice, which I will most certainly follow. If you know of anyone who might be looking for a junior entrant to their business, I would be grateful if you would let me know. Kind regards…"

Next follow them on Twitter if they are on there, and when you have done that put a tweet up about how interesting you found the event and that it was great to meet them and then use their @ names in your tweet. Hopefully as a result of this they will follow you back.

There are some great books on networking which you might

want to read if you are really interested in this subject; I have to say that many opportunities within my own business have come about via networking in this way and it is probably the most productive of all techniques.

The Sales Process – e-shots

Next on the list are e-shots. This means the same email being sent to everyone on your list. Some of the people on your list will prefer receiving emails to letters and vice versa so it's important that you use all methods.

With the e-shot you need to set up a sequence that will firstly introduce you and later on just update and remind them of you.

The first e-shot should go to each person within a day of you meeting them/connecting with them or just identifying them. It should explain who you are and what your career aims are, why you are contacting them, how you would like them to help you and an attachment with your CV and also in your signature a link to a short film of you introducing yourself.

You can use something like Mailchimp for free to do this or even your ordinary email account. Mailchimp will be better if there are large numbers because you can specify a time to send the emails and also you can monitor who opens them. You can also schedule follow-up emails to them. The second, third and subsequent emails need to be updates on yourself. There are templates of all these in in your Action Plan online at www.1stjobseries.com

The Sales Process – letters

Next we have letters. Some people prefer these to emails and, without a doubt, if you want to contact someone senior who receives a lot of emails you are much more likely to get your communication in front of them if you send a letter. They may well have a PA screening their email and post, and many of their emails will be answered by that PA. However, the PA is more likely to retain a letter to show them so it will increase your chances.

Your letter needs to be slightly more formal than your email but broadly speaking say the same. I would suggest that this turns up at their desk a week after the email. It will say similar things about you and request similar things but should have your CV enclosed with a photograph of you on it. The photo needs to be a smart businesslike headshot and not something cut and pasted from a photo of you at a social event for example. The quality of paper needs to be good and it should be nicely folded. Also you must sign it personally in blue ink because research says blue ink is more likely to be responded to than black! The letter must be addressed to them personally and marked private and confidential. Sending second-class post is fine; alternatively you might want to deliver by hand, in which case you can make contact with the person at reception too and hand them your card as well and say this is an important letter that must be handed to the recipient personally. Sometimes you might even achieve an impromptu meeting when you make this approach so please ensure you are dressed for interview if you take this approach (see visits below).

The Sales Process – phone calls

The next item on the list is phone calls which again can be daunting but also can be so very productive that it really is worth your while overcoming any fears and just doing it! Now that you have sent an email and a letter, and maybe in some cases you might even have met the person by now at a networking event, you will have something tangible to refer to in your call. My suggestion is that you write down what you want to say and rehearse it, that you say it with a smile on your face and that you say it standing up. All of these things will help you sound confident and nice to talk to. I would suggest you rehearse every time before you make a call as every call is critical. You never want to be making a call if you feel miserable as this will show in your voice. However, seeing as it might be that you *do* feel miserable, you have to learn a way to snap yourself out of it. The calls must be done if you want to achieve the prize at the end, so standing up, smiling and rehearsing will snap you out of it. Secondly, you need to speak a little more loudly, clearly and slowly than you normally would. You don't want the person at the other end of the phone to be unclear about what you are saying and having to ask you to repeat yourself. You will find that they won't bother with you for long if you are not clear.

The call should go something like this:

"Hi, may I speak to xxx please?"

If you are asked: "Who is it?" just say: "It's John, may I speak to xxxx please?"

If they ask: "John who?" say: "It's John Smith, can you put me through to xxx please?"

If they ask: "What is it regarding?" you say: "It's a personal matter that I need to talk to xxx about please."

If they ask: "Is this a sales call?" say: "No it isn't, it's a personal matter."

Usually, this is enough to get you through. If not, then you will have to speak to the person asking the questions, but hopefully by now you will be through. Whoever it is, you should say the following:

"Hi xxxx, my name is xxxx. I wrote an email to you on xxx and also a letter on xxxx regarding potential career start opportunities within your company and I wondered if you have had a chance to consider them as yet." At this point you will usually find the person you are speaking to has some compassion. Most of us within industry have heard how difficult it is for young people to make a start and so we will give them some time. Next you will probably be asked what it is you want to do or something about yourself. This is where your elevator pitch comes in. You must have a succinct summary about yourself and end it with: "Would it be possible to be considered for an opportunity within your department?"

Sometimes you will find the answer is yes, in which case excellent, we can move on to the interview section, however, usually it will be: "Not yet but please get in touch with my assistant/HR department etc." If this is the case, say: "Certainly, thank you so much for your help, would it be OK to say I have spoken to you and you have referred me to them?" They will say yes and then you have the opportunity to say to them in your next phone call that: "xxxxx of so and so suggested I give you a call." Then you add them to your list in just the same way as all other contacts.

After the call it is important that you follow up with another email and after that a letter. Now that you have made those initial touch points you have to start building them up. Remember the average!

The Sales Process – job applications for specific jobs

Sometimes the person you met or spoke to will suggest to you that there is an open position that you should apply for. Alternatively you may have found the position yourself. Whatever the case, the process of applying for a job will vary considerably. Some of them ask for a letter to be submitted with your CV, in which case refer to the Letters section above and also the template section for letters, making sure you include their job reference. Some might want you to telephone, in which case refer to the Phone calls section above. Sometimes they may ask you to contact the recruitment agent they are using to fill the vacancy. The majority want you to apply online which means you follow their link and complete their online questionnaire. This can be tricky because the questions asked are so varied so it's very important to get someone else to check it for you before you submit it to ensure that you have completed it all properly, and critically that your spelling and grammar are correct.

Many employers put applications in the bin if they contain spelling mistakes and certainly those that put another employer name in because they have just cut and pasted the application from another one! We have seen many of those and they really do annoy the employer!

One of the most important things you need to get across in your application is what you can bring to the job and to the company. Remember my section on CVs and key achievements. Once you have sent the application then the same cycle starts again, i.e. email as a follow-up a week later then a letter a week later then a phone call and so on.

The Sales Process – Twitter and LinkedIn approaches

Twitter is becoming more prolific in business and is a great way of selling yourself. Start with following them as mentioned in the Audience section. Once you have followed them, mention them in a tweet – say things like: "It was great to attend xxx event and to meet @xxx today" or "very interesting to hear @xxx views on xxx in the news today" or "congratulations to @xxx on his new appointment" – all these things will appear on their timeline. They need to be about them and need to be flattering ideally. If they are, you will find that the person will favourite them and/or retweet them. Then they may follow you. Your mission is to get them to follow you. Once they are aware of you, you can message them privately via Twitter saying something similar to your email and also ask if it is OK to contact them via email.

LinkedIn has over 300 million users and is a great way of contacting your target market. You can email them using InMail if you have it or you can ask to be connected if you have a mutual contact. If not then you can find out enough details about them on LinkedIn to then Google and then you can find their email address and phone number that way. Once again you can then make the direct approach as per the Email section above. You can also look at their recent activities on LinkedIn. LinkedIn is great because it will tell you as soon as they have changed their profile or also any anniversaries. For example, it will invite you to congratulate them if they have taken a new job, if they are having a work anniversary, if it's their birthday; you can then make contact by liking their statuses just as you would a friend's on Facebook. You can also congratulate them, which they will like. All this will hopefully incentivise them to connect with you. Once they have, then just like Twitter your updates will appear on their news feed. It's therefore a good idea for you to put industry related updates on your LinkedIn status as for Twitter. For both LinkedIn and Twitter I find that most people are likely to see it if you post very early in the morning around 6am, Saturday morning and Sunday afternoon. This may not be scientific but I have personally tested different times and find the best response is to those posts.

The Sales Process – volunteering

Volunteering to help out with a department or with a new project is a great way of obtaining work experience. As mentioned previously, this may not be an option financially but if there is any way you can make this work then it is well worth making the sacrifice. If you can include in your communications that you are very happy to volunteer your services in order to learn and to demonstrate your worth, it could really help swing your application and will make your letters and emails that much more powerful. Also, if you search 'volunteer' on Twitter and LinkedIn you will probably find a number of opportunities for you to do that. If you do volunteer I would set yourself a personal target of not letting your voluntary status go on for longer than you can afford. For example, if you can afford a month stick to that yourself and make it your goal to add as much value as you can during that month. Write everything down in a daily journal that you do and at the end of that month compile an extensive report of all of it. This will be very impactful and is then something you can send to the manager with a covering letter/email requesting a meeting to review how the month has gone. It will be inevitable that they will agree to that meeting and it's there that you can tell them all the hard work you have put in, demonstrate your value, and then negotiate a paid role. Please see the Interview section to guide you through how that meeting should go.

The Sales Process – referrals from someone who already works there

This is such a powerful part of the sales process and can give you a massive head start if you know how to use it. It is also where Facebook comes in. I haven't mentioned Facebook very much as it is not where you will make many business contacts. However, what you will find is that you have thousands of contacts on Facebook – if not friends then friends and family of friends who work in the industry or an industry related to the industry you want to get into. Therefore you need to update your status on Facebook about your job search and ask your friends to please put you in touch with anyone they know who might be able to give you some advice. Remember you are asking them *to give you advice and not to give you a job*, which would frighten many people off. Now you must be brave and update this status daily for as long as it takes. People will get fed up with you and maybe even take the mickey, but if they are friends they will eventually refer you to someone. Once again the touch point average rule applies, i.e. if you only put that up as a status once, you will get very little response. People either won't see it or will forget about it. However, if you keep adding it there, they will start to think about how they can help you and they will introduce you.

Remember though that very often people are protective of their own jobs and are nervous about giving away any confidential information about their employer. For example, they may know that their employer is hiring and even what the job is, what it is paying and who is interviewing. They may be fearful however of breaking a company confidence. It is therefore up to you to convince them that you will protect their confidentiality and that under no circumstances would you disclose where the referral came from. Remember thereafter that if they do give you some information and a referral then you are in possession of confidential information and you owe that person a huge debt. Under no circumstances can you break their confidence unless they tell you that you can. So once they give you the referral you must treat it just like any other contact you have found by yourself on the internet. The great thing though is that you now have a bit of extra information to help you make that first contact. If the contact is successful don't forget to thank your referrer profusely.

The Sales Process – personal visits

There will be times where a personal visit – just turning up at the company reception – is very worthwhile. Even within our business as a recruiter, we will from time to time go out and pound the pavements within a specific postcode, industrial estate, busy commercial street etc. and pop in individually to each business to introduce ourselves to the receptionist and hand over some corporate information and a letter of introduction. If the receptionist is alone and not busy we will also ask him or her who is responsible for hiring, how many staff work there, are there any vacancies at the moment, do they use agencies, that kind of question. It's amazing what they will tell you. Furthermore it is quite common to be able to convince them to call the person responsible for hiring and for that person to come down to reception to spend a few minutes having an initial discussion.

With all this in mind it really is worth your while doing this too as part of your job search activities. Once again this is daunting and you will be out of your comfort zone. You might feel a bit like a door-to-door salesman and also experience some rudeness or rejection. Please consider doing it anyway and not taking any of this personally. I would suggest that you identify an area where a number of your chosen employers are based, and as with the networking, go out dressed for interview (with comfy shoes on though!) and armed with your CV and cards. Have your elevator pitch ready and be ready to say to the receptionist something like: "Hi – my name's xxx – I don't have an appointment but I am looking for my first job and really would love to work for this company. Could you tell me who does the hiring here and whether there are any vacancies for a junior entrant starting their career?" If you say this with a smile on your face and come across as professional, you will be amazed at how often they treat you very kindly and at least give you information, if not call the person down to speak to you. Be ready to interview! At the very least you can take their card and hand over yours and then you can follow up when you get home with the email–letter–card sequence to them. Receptionists are usually so helpful and you will find that more often than not they will do their best to help you. Often they are the forgotten people within an organisation, they don't get much attention, everyone is visiting to see someone else. So if you are courteous and kind to them and send them professional follow-ups, you will usually find they respond very helpfully indeed and say good things about you to the more senior members of the business if you ask them to.

Summary of the sales cycle

So there we have it – a cycle of activities to lead you to the interview where you will close the 'sale'. Remember that each of these represents a 'touch point' and that on average you need 16 of these before you achieve any sort of result. Once your cycle is clear and you are happy with it, you can start. It is then a simple task of applying the cycle of activities to each name on your list. Leave no more than one week between each activity. This means that your contacts will all receive weekly communications from you until you either get a result or for whatever reason remove them from your list.

You will find this is a huge task – a full-time job in itself – but it will get you results. And what's more it will enable you to build your list even bigger as you meet and add new people to it. This cycle of activities will build your network for the future which will be fantastic for your future career progression when you are seeking not your first job but your second, third, fourth and beyond!

Step 16 – Go to your Action Plan at www.1stjobseries.com and complete the Sales Cycle template that appeals to you – including as many of the 10 items above as you can. You will see there is an arrow running from the last action in the sales cycle back up to the first to produce a cycle of continuous activity. This indicates that the process will be repeated again and again until a result is achieved.

Consistency of the sales cycle

Having 16 'touch points' for each contact on your list may seem like an awful lot of work – and it is a lot of work. The secret is therefore to do some of this work every day – consistently. This really is the key; it's imperative that you do your follow-ups every week otherwise the value of your previous contact is reduced considerably. There really is no point in calling someone once or emailing them once if you are not going to follow up; they are no doubt very busy people and probably receive a lot of communications. Unless you contact them a number of times and consistently they will very quickly forget about you and your applications will be lost among all the others.

Daily timetable

To make sure you fit this in you need to treat this whole process as a full-time job as I said earlier. I would suggest that part of your day every day is to research new job opportunities and the other part is carrying out these activities. Researching new job opportunities can be aided considerably by having job board 'watchdogs' set up. This is where you go on to a job board, complete the form stating what you are looking for, and click the options asking for new jobs that fit those criteria to be sent to you as soon as they are posted. Do this across as many relevant job boards as possible and you will find a multitude of new jobs come into your inbox every day. You can also carry out a Twitter, Google and LinkedIn search every day too. These combined with the watchdogs will give you a strong list of jobs every day to apply for and you will find that your job applications skills improve quickly.

If you are in the position where you also have to work to achieve some earnings, it is very possible to fit in some of these activities around your working hours. Yes it will be more difficult but I want to remind you at this stage that to get the best jobs you have to stand out, work the hardest and do things that others won't be prepared to do.

I would suggest that you aim to devote at least 9 hours per day to 'work' – whether this is carrying out your job search activities or actually doing an interim part-time job to earn some income, or studying to get some more qualifications. Yes this might seem a lot but it still leaves plenty of time to exercise, sleep, relax and socialise and honestly if you are spending any less than a normal working day then you are not taking this seriously. Obviously if you have other responsibilities such as childcare then this just may not be possible. In which case schedule in what you can and adjust your elapsed time frame accordingly. The important point is to make sure that you schedule in as much time as you can and that those hours are spent doing effective things. Don't waste time thinking about what you are going to do during your allocated work slots. Plan them first so that you get maximum effectiveness from your time.

In my experience, no one can expect to achieve great results from less effort than I have described. The more you do, the quicker you will achieve your great result – it is the law of averages!

Last point on this: building up your stamina for hard work

and consistency and commitment now is a fantastic trait for the future. Work ethic is sometimes a lost value yet in my experience it is probably the most distinguishing factor between those who do really well and those who do not.

Step 17 – Go to your Action Plan at www.1stjobseries.com and complete the Daily Timetable template.

Chapter 7

Closing the Sale – The Interview

Obviously the result we want from all this activity is an interview, and an interview is where you secure the role for yourself – or at least 99% secure it. There are some very important points to understand and learn regarding the interview process. Mastering these will hugely increase your chances of securing the job.

The role of the interviewer

Firstly, consider the roles of you, the interviewee and them, the interviewer. Think of it in terms of hunter and hunted. Who is playing what role? Are you the hunter or are they? They will think that they are – they are hunting someone for their role, that's where the term headhunter comes from. Let's look at this another way, though: you are doing the hunting too, aren't you? Therefore you are the hunter and they are the hunted! If you consider the interview in this context, it will automatically increase your confidence and you won't enter the interview feeling like a victim hoping to be chosen. Instead you will feel like the hunter deciding if you actually want to secure this role or not.

Secondly, consider the interview as an information gathering exercise. The interviewer has already gathered information about you and you have about them. At this stage, both of you like what you have found out but you want to find out more. Therefore the interviewer wants to find out about you and your capabilities and suitability for the role – but also you want to find out about the company and their suitability for you too, don't you? You don't want to assume that this is the perfect company for you, because it may not be, and being in a role that is not right for you can be very upsetting. Therefore it's very important that you go into the interview to gather your own information too that will help you decide if this is going to be the job for you. Once again, having this mindset will increase your confidence and also help you to ask the right questions for you.

Thirdly, think about this interview in terms of rapport building, i.e. the interviewer wants to see if you will fit in at their company and in their department – in other words, will you fit into their culture. Also you will want to decide if their culture is going to fit in with you. Do you understand their culture and what they value? Do they value what you value? For example, they might value people who are always trying to be better than their peers, or they might value people who are always trying to support their peers. One is not better than the other, however one will suit you better than the other. These are the sorts of things you need to take a view on as the interview unfolds – will you be able to fit in with and get along with these new colleagues?

Looking at things from their perspective

It's important to put yourself in the interviewer's shoes. How are they feeling and what is their task – what do they want to hear from you? What outcome do they want from this interview?

The answers are numerous.

Firstly, the interviewer is probably a manager at some level and therefore has a lot of responsibility ranging from client responsibility through to operational responsibility and staff management responsibility. They will be *busy*! The reason they are interviewing is probably that they *are* busy! They desperately need someone to fill a position usually. Conducting this interview is just one more thing on their list and they probably have a large list of other things to do that have nothing whatsoever to do with this job role. They may have just received a customer complaint before they came into the meeting, they may have had a staff member resign – other problems may have arisen. Whoever they are, you can safely assume they have got all sorts going on and that this interview is something they want to complete as successfully as they can, as quickly as they can. If it turns out that you are a fantastic candidate, they will be delighted. No one in my experience wants to interview substandard candidates just for fun. No one wants to catch out interviewees – we all just want good candidates. Therefore they are on your side before you start!

Secondly, they have their own personal life outside of work, which once again will be full of activities, priorities, issues, worries, problems, plans that have nothing whatsoever to do with this interview. They are people just the same as you or me. Therefore if they enter the interview looking a bit miserable it will be nothing to do with you. It could be that they have just heard their car needs to have several hundred pounds spent on it, their roof is leaking, their husband or wife has forgotten the food shopping – whatever – it has nothing to do with your interview but it will explain to you why maybe they are not in the best of moods. So long as you are pleasant, smiley and easy to talk to they will soon come round, and they will remember your interview as a positive experience in amongst all those issues!

Besides their own lives and issues which may be affecting their mood, the interviewer will also have concerns that there needs to be a good successful outcome from this interview process. They do not want to be making a mistake and finding themselves interviewing for the same role again in a few months' time. They don't want to get it wrong – and often they are very cautious about getting it right. So what are they worried about? Well, there are a multitude of things and here is a list of some. They are worried that you may turn out to be the employee from hell, i.e. that you will always be off sick, that you will upset other staff, that you won't understand the work or be able to do it, that you will be strange in some way and not fit in. The list goes on and on and although they cannot ask you these questions, you can put their mind at rest by recognising that they have these concerns, and by answering questions in a certain way you can eliminate those concerns.

Finally, they will often not be experienced interviewers and sometimes won't even have been trained to interview. These types of interviewers are the worst because they will lack structure and jump around a bit. They will probably start off with a 'chat' and you will also find that they talk a lot rather than letting you talk. They may ask obvious questions to try to catch you out – and they might ask some standard questions – things like 'sell me this pencil'. Whatever the interview style, you will need to come across as polite and well-mannered and have all your responses ready.

So bearing all this in mind I want to conclude this section by giving you one critical piece of advice. You know much better than they do about you. You know in detail why you would be valuable in that new job within that company and how you can add value. You know why you would be better than any other candidate. My advice to you is no matter what they ask, you must get across in your answers all these points. You mustn't leave that interview without having told them everything you want to tell them. If you find yourself at the end of the interview having not said what you wanted to, then at the end when they ask you if you have any questions just say: "Can I just confirm a few points that we haven't covered please?" and then proceed to tell them what you wanted to tell them! This is your big chance to close the sale and you must not waste it! Be brave!

The interview itself and how to conduct it

You may be surprised that I have left the interview till now. So many people think that the interview is the most important part of the job-seeking process, but as you can now hopefully see, it can often be just a confirmation of what the employer already thinks. Very often the employer has already made up their mind 90% about which candidate they think is going to be the best for the job. So long as you reiterate at the interview what they already know about you, and so long as you look and sound as they had hoped, then it will be no more than a rubber stamp. That isn't to say that the interview isn't critically important but it is certainly not the most important – all the preparation is and that is why I have listed all of that first.

Interviews are often broken down into first and second interviews and sometimes there is even a third. If there is going to be more than one interview they will generally tell you beforehand, and in that case you will find that the first interview is usually a chat and question and answer session whereas the second requires you to make a presentation and meet more people, with a third maybe seeing you being introduced around the department and maybe even being taken to lunch with the team. The rules below relate generally to the first interview and second interview as it is unusual to have a third interview.

Etiquette and behaviour

When you are nervous it is very easy to say or do things that you wouldn't normally do and then create a bad impression. That might be true on the telephone and is especially true in an interview situation. Therefore from the minute you enter the building you must be considering how to put your very best foot forward to create the best impression you can. This is a formal meeting and you really need to treat it formally and not as an informal chat, no matter how friendly everyone is.

Before you walk in, switch your mobile phone off, put it away, make sure you stand up straight and confident and walk in. Walk up to reception, smile and announce yourself clearly and who you are there to see. Make sure you are 10 minutes early and smile!

They will probably give you a badge – which you should wear – and ask you to sit. At the allotted time you will be collected; stand up smartly and smile again, shake their hand, introduce yourself: "Hello I'm Angela Middleton, very nice to meet you," and follow them through. When you are taken into the interview room, do the same again with each of the interviewers if there are more than one and place your coat on the back of your chair and your briefcase on the floor beside you. Ask if you can take some notes and take out your notebook and pen. If you are going for a social media job, have an iPad or an Apple Mac and are a confident user of it, you can actually ask to take notes on that. Please be careful though as it can be very off-putting for the interviewer unless you can take these notes and maintain eye contact in between. I once interviewed someone who did this but they kept their laptop between them and me on my desk and stared into it the whole time taking notes. It was disconcerting and I didn't feel able to engage with them, even though they may have been totally competent and able to do the job. So I would caution this unless you are very competent, can maintain contact, can show them at the end the notes you took, and in that case I would even ask if they are happy for you to tweet about your positive experience in the interview afterwards!

When you are sitting, be sure to just cross your legs loosely at the ankle and keep your hands still in your lap. Try to maintain eye contact and do not slouch, cough or splutter. Do not play with your hair or face and try to keep your hands in your lap other than when you are writing.

You must have in your notebook some questions to ask and you must make sure that the interviewer sees that you have prepared these questions. Open at the page where your questions are written so they can see that you have some questions prepared. This will make you look good and well prepared.

As the interview progresses and you are given information, make a show of writing the information down although obviously not so laboriously that the interviewer has to wait! Just a few shorthand notes is good enough.

Questions to ask and passion

Being super keen and passionate at an interview can make such a difference. I know someone who once appointed someone applying for a senior role despite the views of the rest of the interview panel because when he was asked by a member of the panel why he wanted the job, he pointed at her and said: "That lady there," – which while it sounds cheesy written down wasn't at all in the interview, as he went on to explain how her vision and passion inspired him and matched his own, talked about his moral purpose, and how he wanted to be a part of the transformation. Apparently he turned out to be a great appointment! Do be passionate when you answer your questions!

Also, when you are invited to ask any questions ask them with real interest too. Don't just go through the motions – ask questions that you really want to know the answer to. Those questions could go in the following order:

The industry

The company

The department

The role

Exclude anything to do with hours or pay – unless they volunteer the information do not ask about that, you can always ask afterwards. The important thing to do with your questioning is to demonstrate your interest and passion for the business and the role.

If they have already answered all your questions then tell them that – say: "Actually I have prepared a number of questions but you have answered all of them so thank you very much for that."

Assessment centres

Sometimes it's not just a straightforward interview – you may be requested in addition to attend an assessment centre. This tends to happen with larger corporates and these are usually held over a minimum of a half-day and often over as long as two or three days with overnight accommodation. The very large companies tend to go for the latter. The purpose of these events is to put together a number of shortlisted candidates – often in quite high pressured and competitive situations – to see who performs best. The events will generally consist of tests, group discussions and group exercises and presentations. There will usually be a number of senior people observing all this and rating each candidate. Often you will have up to eight candidates pitched against each other for just one job and often the calibre is very high indeed.

They can be very tough events and the only way to tackle them is to be brave and to go in there in full competitive mode, a bit like the candidates do in *The Apprentice* if you have seen that programme. Having said this, they are not looking for the most aggressive person necessarily – instead what they want is someone who holds their own but can display a range of qualities up against a range of personalities, just as they would during a normal day in the workplace.

In terms of what is being sought, it would usually be competence first and foremost; you need to know your stuff, even if that is just being able to talk about yourself and what you have studied so far – and being able to pass their written tests. Secondly, confidence and presentation skills will be sought. They will also be seeking listening skills; generally speaking those who talk over their colleagues do not do the best whereas those who catch on to what is being said and build on comments around them will be favoured. An ability to think on your feet is useful and will be scored highly too. Picking out and using key phrases, demonstrating your knowledge of the industry and of the company history and future goals, are also very good things to do any chance you get.

Having said all this, there is really no guarantee with this kind of event. All you can do is take heed of the above, hold your nerve, don't be put off by the other candidates who will be often trying to trip you up. Just listen a lot, don't be afraid to speak and focus on putting your best side forward.

You can find a template of an assessment centre overview at www.1stjobseries.com

Presentations

Very often you will be asked to present off the cuff with these types of assessment centres. They will give you a topic and a short while to prepare. The most important thing you can do with this type of presentation is listen very carefully to what is being asked. Look at the information they have given you to prepare with and do make sure that above all else you answer the main question they have asked you to address.

Sometimes though, you will be asked just to give a presentation on a subject of your choice. In this case you should have an industry related presentation at the ready. Ideally have one prepared and rehearsed in your mind that is around five minutes long and certainly no longer. The presentation should contain no more than three key messages and in your mind have five main sections. The first section is for you to introduce yourself and your subject and tell them what you are going to tell them. The second, third and fourth are to deliver your key messages. The fifth point is for you to recap on what you have told them, to thank them for listening and to invite questions. If they want you to prepare slides, then again have those ready in your mind and make sure they are either single bullet points per slide or just a picture, so that they are listening to you rather than reading the slides.

If the presentation is to be about you then the same concept applies in terms of five main points and the three key messages need to be about yourself and ideally with evidence of why you are suitable for this type of role.

Whether you are going to attend an assessment centre or not, having an industry and a personal presentation of this nature up your sleeve to pull out at any time is immensely valuable. You can use rehearsed phrases even during a simple interview and they will really make you stand out.

Template of a presentation at www.1stjobseries.com

At the end of the interview

It is important once they say thank you and stand up to finish that you shake their hand, and after thanking them for seeing you that you tell them you really want this job and ask what would be the next steps. They will probably tell you they are interviewing a few more or that they will be shortlisting for second interview or that you will hear by a specific date. At that point ask them if there is anything that they are concerned about with you at this stage or anything that they would like you to clarify. They will probably say no but if they tell you something then here is your chance to overcome that objection. If for example they say: "Well I am just a little concerned that you don't have enough experience," then here is your chance to sell yourself and convince them that you are a quick learner, your other qualities will make up for this short-term lack of experience and you are a work in progress. If they just tell you that you will hear by a certain date then you can ask if it is OK for you to follow up if for any reason you haven't heard by then. They will tell you that is OK too. Therefore when you leave they will be under no illusion that you really want this job. This is a very important part of the interview indeed because it is surprising sometimes that an employer is not sure if the candidate wants the job and tends to give it to the person who has left them in no doubt. Make sure that person is you!

Once you leave the interview room, your work has not quite finished. Be sure you acknowledge and thank everyone that you met on your way in – smile and thank them for their time, especially the receptionist. They will then remember you fondly and if by chance they are asked their view they will say positive things about you.

Afterwards – follow-up

The last part of closing the sale is the follow-up after the interview or assessment centre. If the interview has gone well – really well – you may have even been offered the job already. Whether you have or haven't, the follow-up will always be the same.

As soon as you are back home, email all the people you met to thank them for their time, tell them that you enjoyed the interview, are very much looking forward to the outcome, and should they require any further information you would be delighted to come along again to provide it. If you were left with any actions from the meeting then reiterate what they are and confirm your intention to complete them and by when. Do not leave it! I have one example where a young very competent person left it for far too long after the deadline date only to be told she wasn't successful. She felt that the assessment centre had gone brilliantly well and knew that she had got on enormously well with the hiring managers. However, she left it for weeks after the deadline before plucking up courage to call them for feedback by which time they had selected another candidate who had narrowly pipped her at the post. If she had shown she was keen enough to chase up during that time, who knows whether the outcome would have been different? The point is she had nothing to lose by chasing up soon and neither do you. Do not be afraid to follow up!

This way you will have done everything you can to close the sale!!

So in summary of this section we have spoken all about you in the context of a product. We have explained that as with every product, it needs to be packaged up as best as can be so that it appears as attractive and fit for purpose as it can be. We talked about visibility and that as with any product the buyer must be able to see it and know where to find it. We talked about guarantees around a product – guarantees that it will deliver. We then talked about the buyer – trying to get inside their head and considering what buying state they are in and what their motivation is. Finally we discussed how you (the product) are in a perpetual state of development, a product in development. The great thing about you is that you are not the finished product. They are buying something that is going to appreciate in value and become more and more useful! How fabulous for them!

Step 18 – Go to your Action Plan at at www.1stjobseries.com and complete the Interview Questions template.

Step 19 – Role play interviews with a friend, colleague or family member and practise all the items above.

Chapter 8

Even when you have a plan things won't always go to plan – expect and prepare to handle this with Emotional Resilience

The previous chapter should have given you enough information to complete your personalised Action Plan and I hope that having that has given you confidence in being able to achieve your goals. It is a series of little steps that enables us to achieve big goals and that is what I hope the Action Plan has given you – a series of little steps for you to take.

Unfortunately though, I now have to prepare you for the worst, which is that inevitably despite having a plan, things don't always go *to* plan! In this chapter I want to explain to you the sorts of things that can go wrong, and to prepare you for this and help you achieve a mindset that takes this in your stride. Think of yourself as a big tanker trawling through the sea. You might suddenly go slightly off course but it is not a problem so long as you recognise it and put yourself back on track each time. If you do that then eventually you will get where you want to go. Here in this chapter I will give you a number of methods for getting yourself back on track.

Give yourself a timetable and diarise it

Now you have your plan and you have decided how much of those 9 hours working time you can afford to spend on this (time when you are not working on anything else) then you must diarise that time. If you don't have a diary then please start using one and I would recommend you make this your electronic diary that comes with your email. This way once you diarise the activities then they will pop up as reminders. I would suggest that you segment your diary appointments to do this work into three-hour slots with an hour in between to rest. Sometimes one of those slots will be taken up with an interview or interview prep or a networking event. Other times it will be taken up with working your list through your marketing plan. The critical thing is to ensure that you keep these diary slots with yourself and don't put them off. Every hour you put into this now will pay dividends in achieving your end goal.

Celebrating achievements – cards and ceremonial ticks!

Your life plan and Action Plan will contain a lot of activities but there will be milestones or key points of achievement. These will range from small ones like 'set up my LinkedIn profile' to 'assemble my first list of 500 contacts' to 'attend first networking event' through to big ones like 'get my first interview', to 'get my first job offer' to 'get my first job' through to 'achieve xx qualification'. Get yourself a pack of small lined revision cards – the ones that you might use as memory joggers if you are doing a talk for example, and write in capital letters your first set of milestones.

It is critical that with the milestone you put a date. This is then a date that you must stick to – a deadline that you really do not want to miss. By having deadlines you will be less inclined to miss a session.

Next write up the card beautifully as you will be looking at it a lot! Then fold it up into a small square and put it in your wallet or purse – something that you use daily. Then every day get it out, look at it and remind yourself of your goals. Soon you will reach the exciting moment when one of your goals is achieved and then you can have the 'ceremonial ticking session'! This is where you get out a coloured pen of your choice and with a flourish you tick the goal off. The aim is that you get to a point where your card is full of ticks and then you can prepare your next card and do the same again. This is how you work through your life plan and your Action Plan and achieve your goals.

It may sound unimportant but it is absolutely critical that you have this card with you all the time. Whenever you feel down, confused or about to give up because things aren't going right and the task seems too big, just take out the card look at the first goal which will be a manageable one and just focus on that next goal and not the rest of them or the big picture. Remember that big goals are achieved by taking a series of small steps.

Don't let opportunities bypass you – keeping your eyes open

Getting a job is a full-time job in itself as I have explained but you need to be doing this with your eyes firmly *open*. It's pointless doing all this work if you are not observant and looking all the time for that little chance, no matter how small, and doing something about it. Whenever someone says: "I know someone who works in that industry who can help you out," *always* follow up. Never feel embarrassed about doing so. If you don't then you will only have yourself to blame. Jobs and opportunities absolutely won't land in your lap and luck doesn't have a chance of happening unless you are open to opportunities.

Stuff will get in the way – don't let it! Doing the important and not urgent things

Inevitably you will not feel like working this plan diligently every day, especially if you are not getting the results you want as quickly as you want. This is where strength of mind needs to come in; whenever something else comes up for you to do instead of your Action Plan, recognise this and ask yourself is this thing *more important* to me than getting my first job and starting my career? Don't ask yourself if it is more urgent or more enjoyable because the answer will often be yes! Remember that the work you are doing here is important rather than urgent. Doing the important and not urgent things will be a key to success for you, not only in your job search but also throughout your career. I know people who left school or college several years ago and are still not on the first rung of their chosen career ladder. This is absolutely *not* because they are not good enough. They are some of the cleverest and most impressive students I know. Also it is not because there are no jobs about – there are, as I have already explained. It is because they are not doing the important things all the time and making their job search an integral part of every single day. This will be critical to your success.

NEXT! You will never run out of leads to pursue so if someone says no, just move to the Next!

Sometimes people tell me that they have tried 'everything'. They have sent off 'tons' of applications etc. and they 'just can't find anything'. I hear that there are 'no jobs'. None of this is true and you can satisfy yourself of this by taking some time to review the market that you want to work in. Start with working out how many companies there are in your industry. Next look up on the job boards how many jobs there are that are advertised in your industry even if they are not suitable for you. Next look up your number of contacts. If you add up all the companies and all the jobs and all your contacts you are going to get to numbers in the thousands. Now assume that you will spend one hour on each of those. That will come to several thousand hours of work. Divide that by 9, assuming you work at job search 9 hours per day, which I am sure you sometimes won't. Every thousand will keep you busy for five months solid. Of course you have the follow-ups to do too, meaning you would want to repeat these contacts and maybe have to do that 16 times on average – 16 x 5 months is 80 – so right there is over six years of work! On this basis there is an enormous amount to do and trust me you will not run out of leads to pursue... and you will always have a *next* one to go to.

Remember no doesn't necessarily mean no forever it just means *not yet*!

How long will it take though – I haven't got months and months

It is impossible to predict exactly how long it will take but from our experience with young people and employers I would say no longer than three months if you are taking this seriously and looking full-time. Your milestones for job search should all be within the three-month period and then your career goals should be beyond that for once you have started your first job.

In order to make sure that this job search does not go on and on there are also some other techniques you should implement.

Measure what works and do more of it

Different things work for different people. You may find that you get much better responses to letters than to emails or better responses to phone calls rather than visits. You need to do a lot of activity over two weeks – even better if four weeks – and then measure the results. If there are more or less equal results then of course just continue as you are; however, if you see a much better result from one method than another then do much more of that. Let's say you are getting your best results from a letter. If that is the case then the next thing is to do a further test on type of letter. Do two or three types in different pen saying slightly different things. Then after a couple of weeks see which letters got the best response. If there is a clear winner then start only using that letter. This is how you will start to get much more value and result out of each activity and thereby become more productive.

You can get even more sophisticated by analysing if you get better results from a certain level of person, from a different time of day or different day of the week. In summary, the more patterns you can pick up, the better, because then you can make sure you focus all your effort into things that are working the best for you.

Ratios

Another important thing to analyse is ratios. It is critically important to ensure that you document every activity you have carried out (you can use the template provided at www.1stjobseries. com) so that you are able to predict what results to expect. After a couple of weeks of activity you might be able to summarise as follows:

- 100 hours spent

- 200 emails sent

- 100 letters sent

- 50 phone calls

- 6 invitations to apply for a job

- 10 referrals to someone else who might help

- 2 interviews

From this you will be able to see that for every 200 emails you send you will get two interviews. Or you might conclude that for every 100 letters sent you will get two interviews. This is very useful because you can then start to focus on how you can reduce that number of letters to still get the same number of interviews. What was it about those two letters that made the difference? Could you make any improvements to achieve more interviews?

As you get better at all this you will start to see those ratios improve and your interview to letter sent ratio for example will improve.

This is very encouraging because you will start to recognise that if you spend a day sending out 100 letters you will at least achieve two interviews. This is how you can start to predict how long your job search is going to take you and is a great way of taking stock of where you can improve your techniques.

Setbacks and how to deal with them

Small setbacks

Please be prepared for a lot of nos and please do not take them personally. Remember what I said about no means not yet, it doesn't mean not ever. Timing is everything!

When you do get a no, try to consider it as a learning experience rather than a setback, even if it doesn't feel like it. When you get that no always see if you can find out why they said no – ask them and list what the answer is. This is an 'objection' and you need to list objections and then practise how to overcome them. So next time you get a no and that same objection you will be better equipped to respond to it and so might be able to turn that no into a yes! Also remember that even if they have said no you are building your connections. So long as you ask politely if it's OK to stay in touch and they say yes then you have added one more person to your network who will now know who you are – especially if you keep in touch. Thirdly you are learning about your industry; if they say no due to a situation at the company then you have learned something about that company and should make a note of it. So you see a no can actually be just a minor setback, which actually is a great learning experience. It can still help you handle objections, build your network and learn about your industry. Sometimes the nos are better than the yeses for that very reason!

Big setbacks

If you have missed your first milestone and you can honestly say the reason is not that you have not spent sufficient time on it, you need to have a review of your activities. Please do not give up at this point – there is *so* much you can do.

Remember the marketing plan and all its components and consider each in turn and whether it can be improved. Firstly the package – you; now that you have all this experience and a better network and knowledge of the industry through your job search activity, can it be improved? This means consider your CV, your LinkedIn profile, your video, your Twitter page etc. – is it time to update and improve these? Secondly the audience – are you approaching the right people? Are they the ones with the power or do they keep referring you to other people in the organisation? If that's the case should you amend your list of contacts and have a revised list? If so then implement that. Thirdly your sales approach. Are some parts of it just not working? For example, are you getting no good responses from your phone calls whatsoever? If so then think about those calls, change your pitch and start making different types of calls.

Everything can be changed at this stage *except one thing* and I cannot overemphasise this. You must *not* change the industry you are targeting. No matter how demoralised you might feel or how much people have made you feel you do not belong and will not succeed, do not change direction. By now you will have accumulated a ton of industry knowledge – more than you know and more than anyone else you know as well. Why would you want to waste all that now? You wouldn't, would you?! What you might want to do though is amend your niche – maybe adjust it a bit or maybe change your location *and* you might at this stage consider further training to get more qualifications. Stephen is an example of someone who encountered this setback. Having studied arts subjects he decided he wanted to work in finance but due to his subjects and insufficient grades he just could not find that first opportunity. He followed our steps and networked significantly as outlined in this book, and someone told him what qualifications he would need to take to get to the first stage. He took another just slightly related job and proceeded then to work every spare hour to pass the first entry-level exams. He failed the first time but studied again and passed the second. He then took and passed the next level *and* he then got the job he wanted. This stuff works if you do it!

Further training considerations

If you are continuously missing out on opportunities due to the lack of a specific qualification, consider again whether gaining this qualification should be built into your Action Plan after all. Before deciding on this course of action, it's important to evaluate properly how much it is going to improve your chances and enhance your marketability. You can do this objectively by looking at job postings online and seeing how many of them ask for the qualification or new skill you are considering acquiring. If you find there are lots then that is a very good reason to pursue it. Another more subjective way is to ask people within the industry whether it is valued. Thirdly – and this is also a very good indicator – ask some recruitment agents what they think is the value of the new skill or qualification, i.e. would it be easier for them to place you if you had it and also how would it impact your salary. If you get positive feedback from all these three sources then it is probably a good idea to pursue the new skill, in which case try to enrol for the course immediately and then build it into your timetable within your 'work' allowance.

Keeping motivated

Another important tool in dealing with setbacks is your physical wellbeing. The way you feel physically has a considerable impact on the way you feel mentally, so if you want to feel strong mentally it is important to feel the same physically. It is certainly the case that when you start taking control of your physical wellbeing and fitness that it improves your mood and helps you become more disciplined and resilient in the other areas too, such as work, so it is well worth maintaining a fitness routine. Once again this should be written into your diary and the appointments stuck to.

The other important aspect of physicality is to be groomed ready for interview at any time so that if all of a sudden you are asked when you can come in for an interview your response is: 'I can come in within the hour.' To be able to do this it means that your hair is always washed and neat, your nails always groomed, males are always freshly shaved or with a neatly kept beard, and that your interview clothes are clean and pressed all ready to pop on at a minute's notice. Don't miss an interview appointment just because your shirt wasn't washed and ironed that day!

It *will* be tough!

Having said all this, know that job search is tough – it is hard work, it is difficult work, and it is tough on you mentally because often you will have to face rejection. Knowing all this and preparing your mindset for it though will help you significantly.

Other people's annoying questions!

Firstly you are going to be asked a lot by well-meaning people: "Have you found anything yet?" This will get on your nerves – a lot! – and it could if you are not careful make you feel miserable. So toughen up and have a standard phrase to respond with every time you are asked. Something like: "Nothing conclusive as yet but I do have a lot of possibilities that I am working on – if there's any referrals you could send my way I'd be really grateful!" That's usually enough for people to say: "Well done," and to wrack their brains for someone who might be able to help you before moving on to the next topic.

Next you are going to have to get used to accepting rejection. Why? Because you have no option but to continue in your search and so you may as well do this positively. Remember that there are *always* going to be more opportunities tomorrow and so what you need to do is to find the positive from each rejection. What are these?

Always take learning points from failure

One head teacher said to me: "Everything teaches you something," and I believe this – we all learn from every experience. No interview is ever a waste of time. If it went badly wrong and you couldn't answer a question then the first thing you can do is look up the answer to it when you get home, rehearse the answer and then you will have learned that thing for the future. Also if there was an assessment centre, a test or whatever that you found difficult, know that if it comes up again you will feel much more confident because it is now familiar and so your likelihood of passing will increase dramatically. When I was seeking my first graduate entry position I remember going for a two-day assessment centre at BP International. I remember that I really wanted that position but found the written tests they gave us overwhelming and couldn't finish them in the allotted time. I was overcome with nerves about the whole thing and as a result I didn't get the position.

A few weeks later though and I was selected for assessments with other parts of that business – BP Oil was one and BP Chemicals was another. The BP Oil one contained a very similar set of tests and this time I finished them all – just. I was offered that job and was happy about it but still went to the Chemicals assessment just in case the offer would be better. At that one we were served up the same sort of routine again. By now I was totally confident – not only had I been on a few assessment centres by then but also I had got used to those types of tests under those types of time constraints. This time I thrashed the tests with time to spare and everything went brilliantly. By the time I returned home they had called my home (there were no mobile phones then) and told my dad that they had never had such high scores and wanted to offer me the job then and there! Now that would never have happened without the experience of several assessment centres. So my point is that if you have a bad interview/test result/assessment centre and suffer rejection as a result then just look at it as great experience, which will help you for the next one.

No might mean 'not yet'

Another advantage of an interview that doesn't result in a job offer is that you have the opportunity of keeping in touch thereafter. They may have decided you weren't suitable for this particular job, however if you keep the door open then that is where the hidden jobs can emerge. By keeping in touch regularly by having them on your list and continuing to work your list, you are on their radar. For example, the first person selected might not work out or they may decide they need to create a second job; I have seen a number of cases where one job becomes two jobs as workload increases within a business.

Rocket fuel

Finally my advice is to use rejection as 'rocket fuel'. I have always done my best work when someone tells me I cannot do it or it cannot be done. Generally speaking, the more annoyed I feel, the greater the dose of rocket fuel to spur me on to take action. So if you feel annoyed with them, just consider that it is their loss. And if you feel annoyed with yourself then remind yourself of the experience you have just gained through that experience and the rocket fuel it has given you.

In summary, even when you have a great plan, things won't always go to plan. If you expect that and know how to handle it then you will have a much greater chance of success because you will be emotionally resilient.

Chapter 9

After the Job Offer –
The First Few Weeks –
Be Indispensable!

The employment contract

The happy day arrives when you are offered your first job – congratulations! It will feel absolutely wonderful and you will want to tell the world and celebrate – which you should – but first it is important to obtain some things in writing and a contract of employment. These should include as a minimum your job title, your hours of work, your pay, your location and your holiday allowance. In addition you should also receive a job description and information regarding any training you will receive. A typical contract and job description are here. Template at: www.1stjobseries.com

Once you have this then you need to accept in writing too. Put a nice letter together confirming your acceptance and email it as well as posting it. Template at: www.1stjobseries.com

Now is the time to celebrate!

The probation period

In your contract you will find that there is usually something called a 'probation period'. This is usually three months and represents a trial period during which time the employer is allowed to analyse your performance and terminate the contract if you don't perform as expected. It is therefore an extremely important and crucial time, so in order to make sure you do pass it you must ensure that you find out what is expected of you during this period, i.e. how will you know if you have done a good job?

Try to obtain in writing the length of the probation period, if it's not already in your contract, when the review date will be and what your targets are during that period. If you know these up front then you can be sure to concentrate on them during those first few weeks.

The first days

It is natural to feel nervous on your first day – everyone does – but remember all the advice for the interview day and continue to implement that. Remember that you were chosen based on how you behaved and appeared then, so more of the same will ensure that you make a good lasting impression.

Punctuality

Firstly you must *never be late* and in fact you should aim to *always be early*. I cannot overemphasise this bit of advice. It is the single easiest thing to do to impress your new employer and to give you maximum chances of success in your career and yet amazingly it is something that so few people do! If you are always the earliest in and always the latest to leave it will not only be noticed by everyone but also you will find that your manager and even your manager's manager will wander over to you at the end of the day and ask how you are getting on, why you are still there etc. Just respond to say that you like to be available to help out with anything extra and to learn as much as you can. It means that you will be noticed more quickly by those higher up the ranks. You will probably find that your colleagues will ask you why you do it and encourage you not to bother. Just smile and say you like to give yourself plenty of time or something like that and make no further comment. Don't only do this for the beginning, do it forever, as it's a fabulous way of making an impression.

Listening and note taking

Above all you must be sure to *listen* and *take notes* all the time. Have a notebook and each day put the date on it and write everything down that you are told. It might seem like overkill and you might think you don't need to because you will remember it, but it will be overwhelming during those first few days, you will be told a lot and you will be expected to remember a lot. You cannot possibly do that without writing it down. Remember that you are currently in learning mode so it will be great also to have these notes so you can refer back to them as the days progress. It really is so annoying for a busy manager if they have to tell you things more than once whereas it is equally impressive if they find they only have to tell you something once and you remember it! If you do that you will be well on your way to impressing already.

During those first few days be very clear at the end of each day what is expected of you tomorrow so that you can plan. Always write under the date the tasks you were set so that at the end of the day you can check back yourself to make sure everything has been done.

Checking in with your manager

It is also really useful to check in with your manager at the end of each day or the beginning of the next. Show him or her the notes you have put together and tell them the work you have done and check with them if they are happy with that and whether there is anything else you should have done or could have done better. Write down any learning points they suggest to you and make sure that you do learn them for the next day. It might seem like overkill to be doing this daily but certainly for the first couple of weeks this is highly advisable and will make sure you set off on the right track.

Keeping a diary and writing a report

Please do ensure you diligently take the notes each day. At the end of the month you will have 20 or 25 days' worth and then you can write up your first monthly report. That report should explain everything you have learned, then everything you have accomplished, including your key achievements, any observations you have and then what tasks you have been set for the following month. It should also talk about what you have enjoyed, who you have met. A template is at www.1stjobseries.com

Once it's done, send it to your manager and any other people you have been working for. They will be surprised and say thank you and probably even that you didn't need to do it. However, it's then safely there as your record of accomplishment. This will become very important for you to produce at your probation meeting and also at any other formal reviews. It will enable you to draw up an accurate list of all your key achievements and you will be very surprised that you have accomplished so much, as will everyone else that you show. It is in my experience the fastest way to impress and to secure promotions. Not many people do this and yet they work so hard. If you do this it will make you different.

I would suggest you prepare these monthly reports for at least the first year.

The importance of managing your manager

This may seem an odd concept when you are just starting out as the office junior. How would you manage your manager? Well, the truth is that if this is done well, it is invisible to them and yet they will be very happy with you. If it is not done at all then they could end up unhappy with you, which you certainly don't want. The concept of managing your manager is really all about understanding them and what drives them and then trying to second-guess what they might need from you.

Firstly a word of caution: your manager is your manager and not your friend. No matter how friendly, nice and supportive they are, no matter if you all go out for office drinks and parties etc., the fact is they are still your manager and so you have to treat them with the appropriate amount of respect and keep them slightly at arm's length. Do not tell them your innermost thoughts, for example, don't tell them who you like or dislike in the company. Be extremely polite, smile and be friendly, always say good morning, always say good night, please, thank you etc., but never cross the line into matey banter. On that note, do be very cautious when socialising with work colleagues too, even if the manager is not present – stories of you will get back. If you are fun to be with but sensible then that will be reported back. If you are the office clown, get drunk, say or do things you regret, your colleagues will laugh along with you – however that behaviour will also be reported back and you may not be trusted any more. Be very careful as it is so easy to damage your reputation before you have even built it properly!

Secondly regarding the manager, consider *their* drivers for a moment instead of yours. They are a person like you and just like you they have a job, a boss, their own deadlines, their own career goals and their own life goals. You are just a tiny part of that – one of their team – and probably the most junior member. If they rush by you one day or seem to give you no time, do not take it personally; they will be probably thinking about all their own issues and you won't have even crossed their mind! What you therefore need to do is to help them achieve *their* goals.

Once you are clear on their goals then you need to align yours to theirs. Your work should always focus on making them look good – also your team. Gradually you need to become the 'go to' person – the one who everyone looks to if something is needed urgently. Even if it starts off with something simple like seeing to the photocopier when it breaks down, be that person. Other things you can do for example include delivering information to them that they asked for before the deadline, or offering to stay late if they look like they are under pressure, and then not go on about it afterwards. This is how you will start to become indispensable, and once you are indispensable you need to remain so.

I have a friend who recently retired from a very successful career in the city where he ended up as Chairman of the largest reinsurance company in the world. He applied for a job as an office junior with an insurance company when he was 15. He came from south-east London and didn't have any special contacts or people to help him up the ladder. At the end of his career he was one of the best-connected people in the City of London. I asked him how he did it and his answer was that he was always first in and last out, he always did all the horrible jobs no one else wanted to do, and he always helped everyone as much as he could. That was his simple advice to climbing the ladder and I believe him. There was no secret besides this.

Your finances

As soon as you start earning do take good financial advice. Find a financial advisor recommended by someone or go into your local bank and tell them how much you are now earning and ask them for some investment advice. If you start putting even a small amount of your earnings into savings now it will build fantastically for your future due to something known as compound interest. This is a very important habit to get into and will give you a nest egg for those times during your career that might not quite go to plan. Also it will enable you to start saving for those things you have identified in your life plan. Put pictures of those with your goals card into your wallet and that will continue to incentivise you to save each month. Even £20 savings per month from the age of 18 could accumulate a substantial amount for you by age 30, so please do get into the habit as soon as you start earning. Also ask your employer about the pension scheme they run, as this will be very important for you to understand for your long-term future.

Your next job

I would caution you to never do a job for less than one year. Even if you decide that it is not the company for you, it really does not look good on your CV to be at a company for less than that period of time. If you end up with two or three companies on your CV where you have worked for less than a year you start to look like a job-hopper, which can put serious employers off. Ideally I would aim for two years before you start seeking alternatives and even then, only do that if you are not achieving promotions with your current employer. Ideally you should be aiming for a promotion every year. If you achieve a promotion at the end of the first year that should be your trigger to stay for a second year. If you achieve another promotion at the end of the second year that should be your trigger to stay for a third year and so on, up to I would suggest seven years or so. At the end of that period consider if your role has changed and whether you might be regarded externally.

Each role and each career path is very different and in the example of my Global Chairman friend he stayed at the same company for over 40 years. That was great for him as he grew with and helped build the company. I do however come across newly unemployed professionals who have been with the same employer for 25 years and when they are made redundant they struggle to find a new position because they haven't developed for years.

Therefore my advice for your onward career is that if you are stagnating within your role and not achieving any sort of progression then perhaps it is time to look elsewhere for your next challenge. If however you are achieving steady progression with your company, if it is growing and you are growing with it then it is well worth you staying.

If you don't like this job

We often see young people enter their first job totally enthused, only to have them contact us shortly after to say they don't like it and want to leave. This is a normal feeling because once you get over the excitement of the new job you start to find you are pushed out of your comfort zone for many reasons. It might be that you don't know the people or you find it difficult interacting with them; it could be that the work is too hard and you don't understand it; maybe you feel silly or awkward asking questions; maybe the work is not difficult enough! We have seen all these examples and more but my advice to you is hold fire and work through these issues – don't leave! We had one example where we received a text from a girl saying she hated her job. Our trainer texted her back to reassure her and encourage her to just bide her time for a bit, that it was early days etc. Luckily she did because just two weeks later she was texting us to say it was the best job ever and thank goodness she'd listened to us!! So always give it plenty of time to adjust. Feelings of discomfort during the first few weeks and months are normal and if you are not out of your comfort zone then you don't grow.

Chapter 10

Some Guarantees, Timescales and How To Apply These Skills Elsewhere

My 100% guarantee

Many ask me if I can guarantee that anyone will be able to achieve a job. Having years of experience in placing all sorts of candidates and particularly young people into jobs, I can categorically say yes. Yes we can guarantee you will find a job – and not just any old job but a job that you absolutely want which will set you on your path to your chosen career. There is a series of IFs though!

The first IF is yes IF you implement all the advice suggested in this book.

Secondly, yes IF you regularly review the results you are getting and amend your actions to make sure that you focus on doing the things that get results and stop doing the things that don't.

Thirdly, yes IF you implement the advice consistently and do so by diarising your activity so that you do some of it every day.

We have placed thousands into their first job and from that I categorically know that those who implement our advice succeed.

This also applies to those needing their next job. I recently helped a lady who had worked in the finance industry for many years as a successful broker. She gave up work to have her child and was off for over 10 years. During that time not only had her own confidence levels regarding work dropped dramatically but also the industry within which she had worked had changed beyond all recognition. Added to that, her personal circumstances had changed such that she was struggling financially and was desperate for a job; however she was constrained regarding location and timings due to childcare requirements. We started off by building her confidence, reviewing her CV, bringing out her key achievements and getting her to recognise the value she could add to any organisation. We then helped her set up her online presence, then her audience, and then her marketing campaign. We taught her new interview techniques and helped her practise those until she felt super-confident. She went for many interviews without success but each time her confidence built because she learned how to deal with various new questions. Then, just as she was thinking she wouldn't be successful, she was offered a temporary position within a local company. This wasn't the ideal job that she was seeking but it ticked enough boxes that she decided to take it. During her first few months she struggled with the new role, the new demands, the new learning points, but she stuck at it and gradually she became more and more indispensable and was made permanent. Fast forward to current time, she has now been there for over a year and has been put forward for an internal promotion into the exact type of job she was originally looking for. I think she will get it but even if she doesn't she will be very well equipped to start applying for those types of jobs as she now has a year of current work experience. She is now applying from a position of strength.

So this story does I believe support my guarantee. Here was a difficult situation and because the lady in question took everything on board that we advised, and most crucially implemented it – in fact I noticed that she was one of the most prolific users of LinkedIn for a while during her job search time – she was able to walk into her desired role, despite all the obstacles.

So yes I can absolutely guarantee that you will get your job if you implement the advice in this book.

Timescales

This is more difficult to guarantee, however what I can do is estimate reasonably accurately that most people if they implement all this advice will achieve their job offer within three months. The first month will be mainly taken up with planning, diarising, reviewing and making mistakes, which they are then putting right. The second month you will be fully in the swing of implementation; if you are following this advice and implementing some of it every day then I would expect during that month that you will have had some interview offers. During the third month I would expect you to be going for interviews and to have secured at least one job offer and probably more. I have numerous examples to support this where individuals secured their first job within a three-month period. I have literally thousands of case studies where this has proven to be the case and some of them are included in the appendix at the back of this book. Take a look at these and you will see the same themes running throughout.

How this approach can improve other areas of your life

Tony Robbins (www.tonyrobbins.com) is a famous life coach who says that when dealing with an issue we should 'see it as it is but not worse than it is'. This is the approach I would encourage you to adopt when you are thinking about your difficulties (if you have them) in finding a job. Equally though, it is a good philosophy to apply to other areas of your life too. These can include your hobbies, your fitness, relationships, material possessions. I have seen that by putting together a step-by-step plan to achieve things and then diarising activities, monitoring what works and doing more of it, generally you will be able to achieve much of what you want to.

Pay it forwards

If you have found the content of this book to work for you, and in particular once you have secured your job, there is no nicer way to show gratitude than to share what you have learned with others. Share it with friends and family, give your time and referrals if you find others in the situation you were in when you couldn't find a job. You will find that this gives you as much fulfilment as securing things for yourself, and what's more, you will no doubt come into contact with those people at later stages in your life when maybe they can help you too.

Step 20 – Once you have your job and if you believe this book helped you to achieve that – then please do refer the book to someone else who needs this advice!

Wishing you a wonderful career – after all your hard work you deserve it and with continued effort you WILL achieve it. Who knows you may end up as their Global Chairman like my friend did!

PART 3
TOOLS

This section is designed mainly to provide some guidance and examples of the most useful templates mentioned within the book. All the latest versions of the templates can be found on www.1stjobseries.com where you can update them online and then save them/print them off for your own use.

Chapter 11

Purpose of your CV

There are thousands of articles and advice on what should go into a CV, how long it should be, how it should look and so on. I can give you my own view here and it is based on what I have seen work over the years. Before I show you a template, consider the purpose of the CV. It is usually to secure you an interview, isn't it? Therefore you need to consider what will be most likely to achieve that. The answer is usually that your CV contains relevant experience and/or skills, that you have made some remarkable achievements and that you appear to fit other criteria, which can vary hugely. Rightly or wrongly, employers do make decisions to interview based on CV. Therefore it is vital that it contains all the information they need and that it convinces them that they want to meet you.

Bearing in mind the purpose we can now be clearer on the content.

Content of your CV

Summary, Skills and Qualifications, Work Experience, Key Achievements are the four most important headings. All the other information relating to hobbies, address, references etc. do of course need to be there but what you say under each of the above four headings will be the deciding factors.

Summary

This must explain in just a few sentences what you are seeking and why you would be of value to an employer in that field.

Skills and Qualifications

A list of these in order of most recent first – with grades and with the place (school/college etc.) where you took them. Skills don't have to be examinations by the way; they can include driving, languages, proficiency in a particular sport etc. These things are much better positioned here rather than in the hobbies section. List them in order of what is relevant to the job first. If you are not sure then always put the driving skill as the first one and the languages as the second, followed by the others.

Work Experience and Key Achievements

These must be of relevance to the job you are interested in applying for. Therefore if you are seeking a role in finance for example, then you would want to put a key achievement that relates to that field. Your key achievements must be quantifiable. Rather than saying 'I spent four months helping to set up a new business' and just listing your tasks, you would say 'I spent four months helping to set up a new business during which time I implemented processes which saved one hour per day or saved £x per month'. Achievements are always best from an employer perspective if they can be linked in some way to the saving of time and money or the generation of revenue for their business.

Other points regarding content include:

Photo – This should be a professional headshot and I would suggest you put it at the top right of your CV. The same headshot should be used on your social media profiles rather than a variety of different ones.

Truthfulness – We have all heard cases where executives in high-powered jobs have suddenly lost their job because their CV was found to be untruthful. Please let that be lesson enough to you to ensure that your CV always contains the truth. If you wish you can leave out things that don't show you in the best light but what you must not do is put anything in it that you cannot substantiate.

Do not make up skills or experience, do not exaggerate grades; all these things can and usually will be double checked and you do not want to lose out on a job offer if things you have claimed turn out to be untruthful. One of the biggest concerns of an interviewer is that the person in front of them is trustworthy. If they find them not to be then they will most certainly not hire them – ever.

Gaps – It is inadvisable to have unexplained gaps in your CV. Readers will instantly be suspicious and wonder what you were doing during those gaps. It is best to be very honest about gaps in between jobs.

Length of your CV

There is much debate on this but I would suggest that you keep it to two pages. One page feels too short. More than two pages is definitely too long. So I would space it out with reasonably large print over two pages.

Many say that you need several versions of your CV but I would argue against that. You want to be absolutely happy with your CV and totally familiar with it when you are being interviewed. Imagine if you are unsure what CV the interviewer is looking at for example! My recommendation is to have one version of your CV that is as excellent as possible. Then refine it as you go along – this keeps things simple for you and ensures that you put all your efforts into that one CV.

Template of a good CV is below but we update these regularly so for the very latest version go to www.1stjobseries.com

First Name Surname

Tel: Mobile then landline number

Email: professional email address

Summary

4–5 sentences: A brief overview of your unique attributes (soft skills), background, and summary of what you are doing at the moment and your future career aspirations (please see below as an example to use):

My current goal is to complete my Traineeship Programme and to progress on to a 12-month work placement and start my apprenticeship in Business and Administration.

Key Skills

Examples of hard skills such as ICT, languages, problem solving, team working, subject knowledge etc. in bullet points and then columns.

Training

Any training such as pre-apprenticeships, outdoor pursuits, First Aid, computer training etc. in chronological order. Example below:

- 6 weeks Traineeship Programme at MiddletonMurray
- Workskills and Employability
- Customer Service
- 12 Steps to Recruitment

Also take this opportunity to share any additional achievements that you are proud of, e.g. Prince's Trust, Duke of Edinburgh Award.

Education and Qualifications

6th form, college, secondary school – dates started and finished and name of establishment, again in chronological order. Example below:

A-levels

GCSEs

**North West Kent College
September 2011 – November 2011**

**Blackfen School for Girls
September 2006 – June 2011**

Work Experience and Key Achievements

A brief overview of your work experience including where it took place, duration and skills learned from the experience, again in chronological order. Example below:

Start Date – Present

MiddletonMurray – 6-Week Traineeship Programme

Training and work skills covered:

- Telephone answering workshop
- Different methods in applying for jobs
- How to construct a covering letter and professional CV
- Researching, creating and delivering PowerPoint presentations
- Public speaking
- Confidence building
- Following instructions
- ICT skills – use of Microsoft Word, PowerPoint & Outlook
- Working in a team and individually
- Working to deadlines and prioritising workloads

Employment History

If you do have any previous employment history then state it here starting with your most recent employment, state month and year, job role, activities/tasks. If not then leave this out.

Hobbies and Interests

Open with words like: In my spare time I enjoy...

References

Available upon request or put names of teachers or relevant ex colleagues with whom you have worked.

Chapter 12

Your Communication Methods

Covering letter

Your covering letter is where you can distinguish yourself and bring out the points in your CV that are very relevant to the job you are applying for. It should expand on your personal summary in the CV.

Letters are now sent on a less and less frequent basis – so if you send one to a future employer it will make you stand out. You do however want to stand out for the right reasons! Therefore the quality of the letter must be exceptional. It goes without saying that the spelling and grammar must be perfect and so must the layout of the letter. Besides that it is advisable that the quality of the paper and of the envelope is good and that the letter is folded neatly into three. Use a first-class stamp and do make sure that you send it the day after your interview at the latest, the same day if possible. This will impress the interviewer and if they are torn between yourself and another candidate it may be enough to sway them over to you. So do take the time and effort to do this.

A template of a letter is below, however we update these regularly so for the most up-to-date version go to www.1stjobseries.com

COVER LETTER TEMPLATE

EMPLOYER'S ADDRESS

EMPLOYER'S FULL NAME

YOUR FULL ADDRESS

TODAY'S DATE

DEAR (PERSON'S NAME OR DEAR SIR OR MADAM IF YOU ARE UNSURE)

RE: *(name of position/vacancy – including vacancy number if applicable)*

I am writing to apply for the position of *(position title)* at your company which was advertised in *(name of newspaper/on name of website etc.)* on *(date).*

Having extensively researched your company's values and services, I was especially interested in *(state the type of position and why you are interested in it and link this to your past experience and your key skills that are relevant to the job if you can).*

I have enclosed my CV to support my application. It shows that I would bring important skills to the organisation including xxxx *(list ones that are relevant to the job).* At *(school/previous job)* I carried out duties such as xxxx. I am keen to develop my skills and always willing to undertake any training required to adapt to the needs of the business.

Add a paragraph to give the employer more information about how you match the job they are advertising. It is also good to show that you have some knowledge of the company with whom you are seeking employment and the role you are going for, so do a little research and use the information about the company, which has been provided in the job description.

I would enjoy having the opportunity to talk with you more about this position and how I could use my skills to benefit your organisation and very much hope to hear from you. Thank you in advance for considering my application.

Yours sincerely *(when you know the person's name, e.g. Dear Mr xxx).*

Yours faithfully *(when you don't know the person's name, i.e. Dear Sir/Madam).*

Sign your name

Print your name, telephone number and email address

Your email address

You need a professional email address. Try to buy the domain of your name – in my case I have purchased www.angelamiddleton. com – if you cannot get that try using your middle name or a .co. uk domain or a .me domain. These are usually quite cheap to buy. Once you have them, set up your email address as your first name at the domain. For example mine is angela@angelamiddleton.com This not only looks professional but it is easy to remember and also it is future-proof by which I mean that it does not have a year in it nor does it have any reference to nicknames that I might want to shake off in a few years!

Your emails

Your emails should always be written professionally, as you would a letter with Dear xxx at the beginning and Yours sincerely at the end. Full grammar rather than shorthand should be used. Also you need to have a signature at the bottom which is fixed and can contain a link to a video of you introducing yourself, your Twitter and LinkedIn pages, there can be a message in it and even a photo of you. At the very least it needs to contain your name and your telephone number so that people can contact you quickly. Your emails must add to your brand and strengthen it, they must not detract from it in any way, so be very careful with all emails that you send.

Your voicemails

Firstly please do consider the tone and sound of your voice. Most people when they are a bit nervous speak more quietly, more quickly and more high pitched. Therefore you should focus on ensuring that your voice is clear, loud (but not shouting!), slower than usual and deeper than usual. Check your voicemail message on your phone. Don't leave it as your phone provider's answerphone, but equally please do ensure that you have a well-worded and clear message for any callers. Write it down and rehearse it and re-record it until you are happy with it. Something like: "You have reached (your name). I am sorry I cannot take your call right now but please do leave a message and I will call you back as soon as possible. Many thanks for calling," is perfect. You must make sure you listen to your messages though! Voicemail is not as popular with young people as it is with older people so you must get into the habit of listening. Not calling back the same day really does not leave a good impression, so aim to call back within the hour if you can.

Equally if you are calling someone about a job, do leave voicemail, don't just hang up. Something like: "Hello (their name), this is (your name) calling in connection with the letter I sent you about possible job opportunities. I would be very grateful if you or your assistant could call me back on (your number). Many thanks for your time." Once again, have this written down and rehearse it before you leave the message; if you are unhappy with it you can often re-record your message so take advantage of that facility too if you need to. Obviously, do leave a number for them that you can always answer; don't leave a number that possibly other people might answer.

A pay-as-you-go phone to be used specifically for this purpose is a good idea if you don't already have a mobile phone.

Business cards

You can go online and order very cheaply or free some business cards for yourself which should contain just your name and mobile number and email address. Make them as plain as possible – fancy colours and fonts are only suitable if you are seeking work in the creative industries and even then you may be judged negatively on them. Therefore play safe with these. They are for you to leave with people at networking events, at reception desks if you visit offices or to clip to your CV.

Application forms

It is difficult to advise what to put in these as they are generally so diverse. There are however some general rules that apply to all:

- Perfect handwriting

- Exact extracts from your CV – certainly no contradictions

- Stick very strictly to the number of word rules, e.g. if they say 500 words give 498 words and not more but not much less

- In any sections where free format writing is requested make sure that every statement can be backed up by facts. For example, 'I am hard working' needs to be supported by some facts to substantiate it. Remember that all your competitors will say similar things so yours needs to stand out with facts and proof rather than generalist statements

- Timeliness – ensure that the application form is delivered within the deadline

- Covering letter – if there is a covering letter then try to not duplicate what you have put into the application form but do refer to the various sections in the form

- Make sure you keep a copy!

- Make sure you complete all sections

Chapter 13

Your Online Presence

Be careful!

If you are seeking your first job then this is the time to transform your social presence from just a social presence to a professional one. Social media can be a fantastic platform for you to let the world know about your skills and that you are seeking your first position. Do not be shy about this! The more people who know that you are looking, the more likely it is that you will receive help from someone who can influence your chances. Having said that, you do need to be careful and ensure that when people look at your online presence they are presented with a professional image. Often this step is missed by young people and can be their downfall with a job opportunity and they may not even realise it. Whenever I interview someone for a position I check out their online presence after the interview to check that it matches up to what they have said at interview. There has been more than one occasion where what I have been told does not match up with what I have seen on their Facebook for example and consequently they have not been offered the position. Don't let your online presence trip you up like this – instead let it become a tool that increases your chances of success!

Principally I am talking about LinkedIn, Twitter, Facebook and Instagram here (the latter less so). In just the same way as your CV needs to sell you, so do these profiles. Take a look at them at the moment, would you hire you based on what you see? If not then do something about it well before you start sending out your applications and inviting people to find out about you.

Facebook

With your Facebook (even if you no longer use it very much) I would suggest this is reserved for your personal use and that you simply lock down all the privacy settings so that only your friends can see your content and not friends of friends or the public. Also I would suggest you audit your list of friends and remove anyone you don't know and trust; you just don't know who they know and who they could show your content to. Facebook change their privacy settings often so this is something that you should do regularly.

One thing I would say however is that Facebook is a rich source of referrals if you ask for them. Update your status regularly about your job search, how you are getting on, keep on asking for more referrals. Sometimes people need to see this a number of times before they are called to action and, as we know, not everything you write is seen by everyone so if you update at different times of day and night then it is more likely that all your friends will see this at some stage.

Your profile picture

Ensure that your profile picture is one that you would not be embarrassed for an employer to see. One of you achieving something would be great but otherwise just a nice friendly headshot. Avoid any where you are out socially – keep those for within your Facebook. Don't wear sunglasses in it, no pouting or pulling faces, making signs with your hands etc., just a nice clear picture that looks like you!

LinkedIn

You may not have a LinkedIn profile as yet. LinkedIn is like Facebook for business people. Basically you connect with people and then they are known as first connections. Then all their connections are known as your second connections. Unless they lock those down, you can look at all their connections and invite them to connect too. You can search all your connections for key words, meaning you can use it to find out names of people who do particular types of jobs, for example. In the same way, anyone on LinkedIn can search by key word and employers and recruiters often do. You may come up in their search if you have the right key words that they are searching for in your profile. Also jobs are advertised on LinkedIn, and you can direct message your connections. There is a feed so you can see latest news about people's new jobs, their anniversaries of jobs and of course their status. You can update your status as with Facebook, you can add photos and documents, as well as presentations etc. You can follow companies and you can join groups. For someone starting out in their career as well as building their career it really is an important tool and is second only to your CV in demonstrating your skills experience.

It is very important that your LinkedIn profile reflects exactly what is on your CV, i.e. they must not clash. You can use some of the wording of your CV and build on it. You can attach your CV. On a daily basis spend some time on LinkedIn, adding your contacts that are already on your list and also reviewing and adding their contacts. You should make sure that you use key words in your profile that relate to the industry you want to get into to maximise your chances of appearing if employers or recruiters are searching for people in your chosen industry.

Update your status daily with your progress on your job search; this will ensure that you keep on appearing on the news feed of your connections and this in itself might achieve some job opportunities for you. Make sure your updates are placed at different times of day and night and also over the weekend; do maximise your chances of your updates being seen by as many of your connections as possible. Set up saved searches of jobs so they appear on your news feed. Join groups relevant to your industry. Follow companies that you would like to work for. All of this will help build your online presence and build your network for the future.

Go on to www.linkedin.com and search for Angela Middleton to see my example profile.

Twitter

As with Facebook, you may already have a private Twitter account that you use to communicate with followers and those that you follow. Once again, look at this as if you were a future employer. What does it show and say about you? If there is anything that you wouldn't want an employer to see about you then shut it down and set yourself up a more professional one. Certainly if the Twitter handle that you have is not professional sounding, then set up a new one. As I have already stated, Twitter is a great place to build your audience of employers that might hire you and it is also a great place to display your ever building knowledge of the industry by tweeting new things you have discovered or heard that day and by updating people on your job search. As with LinkedIn, the more people who see you are searching, the better. On your Twitter profile do ensure you leave your email address and a summary about the type of career you are seeking to build, also put a link on there to your LinkedIn profile. Remember that when you update status on LinkedIn you have an option for it to update Twitter automatically too. I would suggest you switch off that option due to the 140 word limit on Twitter constraining what you want to say on LinkedIn, and just do separate updates on each. Never use this Twitter account for comments regarding social life; you are building a professional profile here so don't let it slip. Also do retweet things you have found out or think are good. Be generous with what you share, and support and encourage those you follow rather than just talking about yourself. This will help you engage with more followers.

Go to www.twitter.com and search for Angela Middleton to see an example profile.

Instagram

Instagram is still the least used of social media for business. If you have an Instagram channel with followers then as with Facebook do make sure that it is private, and secondly do announce to your followers that you are seeking a new role. Once again, you may well find that they know someone who can advise you or refer you.

Video (YouTube)

Producing a video of yourself speaking to the camera is still an unusual way of promoting yourself but can be very impactful and you can set up your own YouTube channel using your name to display it on.

We have prepared videos for several young people we have helped.

These can be done very simply using your mobile phone. They should normally just be a headshot position and the best ones will show you in business dress explaining what sort of position you are seeking and why an employer should hire you. They really shouldn't be longer than a minute. The great thing about this type of video is that you can rehearse it as many times as you wish until it's perfect and then you can add it to your profile, meaning employers and recruiters can get to see you before they invite you for interview. Bear in mind that research shows that employers make their hiring decisions based only 10% on what you say and the rest is about how you appear and how you say things (stats mention ability to hold eye contact, personal appearance, strength of handshake as all being extremely influential on the decision). Therefore if they like what they see and hear they might then invite you for interview, even if what they see on your CV is not exactly what they were looking for. Of course you do run the risk with this that they don't like what they see and hear and so it causes them not to invite you for interview – but then in that case you would have been unsuccessful at interview anyway so it is best to find out beforehand and not waste your time.

Chapter 14

Interview questions for you to ask

Here are some questions for you to ask but you can find loads more at www.1stjobseries.com

THE COMPANY

1. What is it about the company that makes people want to stay/made you join and stay?

2. How does the company encourage a coming together of staff through activities?

3. What is the company renowned for within the industry?

4. What position does the company hold in the marketplace?

5. What are the company's plans for the future?

6. What is the company's current annual growth rate?

7. How has your recent merger/takeover altered the company if at all?

8. How many offices are there?

THE DEPARTMENT

9. What exactly does the department do in terms of the overall company?

10. What are the department's plans for expansion?

11.What are the ages of the people in the department? What age group are the other members of the department?

12.What is/are the personality/ies of the people I would be working for/with?

13.How closely does this department work with other areas of the company?

14.How does this department compare in size to others within the organisation?

15.To what extent do you encourage staff to interact between departments?

TRAINING AND APPRAISAL

16.What sort of training is offered to staff within the department?

17.Is training provided in-house or are courses held externally?

18.What training facilities are available within the department/ company?

19.What encouragement is given to further study?

20.How often do you hold meetings to assess the skills/abilities/ progress of staff?

21.Who will I talk to about my progress and how often will this take place?

THE JOB

22.How would you describe a typical day for the person doing this job?

23.What would I have to do for you to feel I had done a really good job?

24.What systems do you use?

25. Who is doing the job at the moment?

26. What sort of handover will there be with the person who is currently doing this job?

27. Why did the last person leave? Were they with you for a long time?

28. What percentage of my job would be typing and what percentage would be administration?

29. You have asked for someone with good PowerPoint/Excel skills. How big a part does this play in the role? To what extent would I use my PowerPoint/Excel skills?

30. What type of person are you looking for to fill this role?

31. What competencies are you looking for the new person to have?

32. Who would I be reporting to?

33. How long has the person I will be working for been here?

34. How long have you been here?

35. How long would you expect a person to stay in this role?

36. Will there be the opportunity to become involved and work on my own initiative?

37. If I am keen to develop the role what would you like done?

PROSPECTS

38. What structures are in place for career development?

39. What are the promotional prospects? What prospects are there for career progression?

40. If I begin as a junior now, where could I hope to be within the company in 5/10 years' time?

41. How do you encourage staff to progress within the company?

42. How do you see this role developing?

43. What are the long-term development opportunities for this role?

44. What is the process for advertising jobs internally?

INTERVIEW PROCESS

45. When can I look around the department where I would be working?

46. When do you think you will decide on your shortlist for second interviews?

47. How many more people do you expect to interview for this position?

48. When do you expect to be able to make a decision?

SPECIAL QUESTIONS ON INTERVIEW PROCESS

1. When are you looking to take someone on board?

2. If you were interested in my application, when is the position to start? When are you looking for the selected candidate to start?

3. What is the next step from here?

4. What further interviews are proposed for someone successful at this stage?

Questions you might be asked

This depends on the job you are being interviewed for. Broadly speaking they fall into the following categories:

Competency questions

These are questions relating to the industry and job itself or to other areas, such as hobbies. You will only be asked these if you have claimed to have experience, knowledge and skills so please do ensure that you only say you have experience, knowledge or skills that you truly do. Don't exaggerate otherwise the interview is the place where you will be found out! I once wrote on my CV that I enjoyed current affairs and was asked by the interviewer what I thought of the devolution of Scotland and the Corrie bill on abortion, which were apparently in the news that week. I knew nothing of either and consequently failed the interview, so do beware!

Template competency questions at www.1stjobseries.com

Scenario questions

These are questions asking you to describe what you would do in a certain situation. They are expecting you to draw on expertise and knowledge although I always think these types of questions are also a good judge of someone's imagination. It is very difficult to advise what these questions might be but it could include things like 'how would you deal with a situation where you were in conflict with your colleague?' These are very difficult questions to know how to respond to and the trick is to consider how the employer might want you to behave in that situation and then respond accordingly. Remember that the employer has a whole series of concerns that they want to eliminate. They don't want to hire those who might cause conflict, go sick, upset others, be lazy, not grasp things quickly enough etc., so make sure that these questions give you a chance to describe how you would be just the opposite.

Questions about you

Obviously you know yourself well and so you will know everything about yourself there is to know. Nevertheless, if you are asked to tell the employer about yourself you should still have your elevator pitch ready.

Elevator Pitch: (when asked to "Tell me about yourself")

Starting point: You need to have a start/beginning, state your name, age, where you live, which school you attended and what you achieved there by telling them how many GCSEs you gained and if you have grades A-C then highlight the key subjects such as English, Maths and ICT. Talk about any additional activities you did such as part of the school football team or football team outside of school, other sporting activities e.g. the Duke of Edinburgh Award. Again you are thinking about telling them your USPs: unique selling points!

Middle point: You then need to explain what you did next after leaving school, so talk about your unpaid work experience or employment, what skills and duties you performed while there and that you can bring these skills to your next job.

Ending point: Now tell them what you as a person can offer that employer, how you can benefit or add value to their company, why you are right for their role. Finish off by thanking them for listening.

Template elevator pitch at www.1stjobseries.com

MIDDLETONMURRAY APPRENTICESHIP CASE STUDIES

Toni Ann's perseverance pays off!

Apprentice of the Month – Toni Ann Francis – Nov 2014

Overcoming all the odds, perseverance through some tough times, dealing with shyness, constantly demonstrating professionalism and being calm under pressure were some of the personal and professional attributes that saw Toni Ann Francis, an Office Assistant at Barnet-based Bandana Ltd, being named as the winner of the MiddletonMurray 'Apprentice of the Month' Award for November.

The Award, which is chosen by a panel of judges that includes Tessa Oversby, Head of Employability at Barclays Bank Plc, Peter Varney, CEO of KEH Sports Ltd and Vice Chairman of Ebbsfleet United FC, Steve Sutherland, Head of Marketing and

PR at MiddletonMurray and MiddletonMurray CEO Angela Middleton, is designed to increase the awareness of the benefits of employing apprentices to prospective employers and to highlight to young people that while working in a paid job as an apprentice they would gain valuable experience and confidence, plus a recognised qualification.

It's always a difficult task choosing the winner from the consistently outstanding nominees and this month was no different. The achievements of the other nominees were very impressive. The judges felt that **Luke Reinbach** of MiddletonMurray's Romford office is clearly doing a great job and is 'one to watch' and they gave a special mention to **Curtis Carrasco** of OCS as the company are considering making the job he is undertaking a permanent position in the structure and one which they will be encouraging him to apply for formally. However, the judges felt that Toni Ann was thoroughly deserving of the Award this month.

Summing up the judges' decision, Steve Sutherland said: "*Toni Ann's story is a compelling one which graphically highlights that with dedication, hard work and support you can achieve your goals. To be so highly regarded by her MD for the job she is doing despite dealing with, and overcoming, difficult personal circumstances is admirable and speaks volumes about her character.*"

Proscovia Kasozi, Toni Ann's assessor at MiddletonMurray, who nominated her for the Award said: "*Toni Ann has overcome all odds to achieve this qualification; she has persevered through tough times, she has dealt with shyness and now blossoms with confidence. She had a very bad experience in her first placement while she was dealing with personal circumstances and spent a lot of time with our Safeguarding Officer Dawn Mason but she never gave up on her qualification.*"

Proscovia continued: "*Throughout my visits, Toni Ann has demonstrated her professionalism; she is always willing to learn, she supports her team and works extremely well under pressure. Most of her colleagues have commented that she has a calming influence in the office. I am delighted the judges have chosen her for this Award.*"

Speaking at the presentation of the Award which was made by Maria Darbin, MiddletonMurray's Performance and Quality Manager, Toni Ann said: *"When I started training with MiddletonMurray I didn't have much confidence, I was quite shy and didn't like interacting with people. With the help of MiddletonMurray I have come out of myself and I'm now fully able to interact with people and not feel inadequate. I have gained so much by doing this qualification and feel it will carry me a long way in the future."*

Angela Stone, Managing Director of Bandana Ltd, pictured here with Toni Ann said: *"Toni Ann is the first person people see when they visit our offices. She always greets people with a confident, warm smile. She is softly spoken, calm and always extremely polite and she carries out her duties very professionally. Toni Ann is a pleasure to have around and we hope she stays with us for a very long time."*

Kenny's hard work pays off

Apprentice of the Month –
Kenny Lee – October 2014

An outgoing and cheerful personality, with an infectious sense of humour; professional and calm in his attitude to his peers, management and people in general and helping to create a good team ethos at work were just some of the stand-out attributes that saw Kenny Lee, a Deployment Co-ordinator at OCS Retail Support, a division of OCS Group UK Ltd, being named as the winner of the MiddletonMurray 'Apprentice of the Month' Award for October.

As is always the case, choosing a winner from the consistently outstanding nominees is a difficult task and this month the judges were very impressed with the achievements of **Olivia Biddiss** of CER Financial Ltd, **Brogan Slade** of the Children's Heart Foundation and they gave a special mention to **Hamza Madih** of Austin Dean Recruitment. However, the judges felt that Kenny was thoroughly deserving of the Award this month with Peter Varney even suggesting that MiddletonMurray *"should use Kenny's story as a case study!"*

Summing up the judges' decision, Steve Sutherland said: *"All four of the nominees this month have done exceptionally well, however we all agreed that Kenny Lee has performed brilliantly and he has clearly grasped the opportunity with both hands and has been offered a permanent position at the end of his apprenticeship, which says it all really."*

Steve continue: *"The judges were also extremely impressed by the quality of the nominations produced by the MiddletonMurray assessors who provided us with such an in-depth and informative nomination forms."*

Jan Donegan, Kenny's trainer/assessor at MiddletonMurray said: *"From the outset, Kenny has had a professional attitude towards his apprenticeship and the work produced is consistently to a high standard and on time. This applies not only to his course work but also to everything he produces for his employer. Kenny has grown in confidence in his job role, where he has taken on many new challenges willingly to become an important and competent member of the scheduling team at OCS. Kenny has been offered and has accepted a permanent position to start once his apprenticeship is completed. This is very well deserved."*

Natalie Day, Deployment Manager at OCS Retail Support said: *"Kenny's outstanding contribution to OCS and his continued efforts have been truly appreciated; he has proved himself to be a valued member of my team. It is important to celebrate success and recognise achievement and we are delighted that Kenny has been awarded 'Apprentice of the Month'. We are also thrilled that Kenny has accepted a permanent position with OCS and I look forward to helping Kenny develop and progress further within the business."*

Speaking at the presentation of the Award which was made by Maria Darbin, MiddletonMurray's Performance and Quality Manager, Kenny Lee said: *"I was surprised and honoured to have been nominated as 'Apprentice of the Month' and was over the moon to hear that I had won. I have enjoyed my apprenticeship at OCS where I have learned a lot and am delighted to have been given a permanent job here. I am very grateful to MiddletonMurray and OCS for giving me this opportunity."*

Frankie goes to... a permanent position!

Apprentice of the Month – Frankie Mitchell – Sept 2014

A confident and professional attitude, a friendly personality with a calm approach and being a great role model to other apprentices were the main qualities that resulted in Frankie Mitchell of Tay Associates being named as the winner of the MiddletonMurray 'Apprentice of the Month' Award for September.

Choosing a winner from the Award nominees is becoming harder and harder each month with September being no different as the judges were very impressed with the achievements of **Olivia Biddiss** of CER Financial Ltd and **Nikita Gibson** of Pimlico Plumbers. However, the judges felt that Frankie was the stand-out candidate this month as explained by Peter Varney: *"Frankie has clearly blossomed over the past 11 months and has made recommendations for improvements at Tay that have been accepted. He has proved so good at his job that he has been taken on permanently, which is exactly what the objective of any apprentice should be."*

Jan Donegan, Frankie's trainer/assessor at MiddletonMurray said: *"I'm delighted that Frankie has won this month's Award. From day one, it was clearly apparent that Frankie and Tay were an ideal match and he has consistently produced good quality work. It is very well deserved and he has worked hard to achieve it, setting very high standards for the two new apprentices he is now mentoring at Tay!"*

Susanna Tait, Managing Director of Tay Associates said: *"Tay is a fast-paced, award-winning recruitment business servicing London's most prestigious employers. Frankie stepped into what was a new role for Tay, which has required him to work closely with the senior management team. He has contributed a number of very valuable ideas, many of which have resulted in the implementation of improved systems and procedures for the company."*

Susanna continued: *"Frankie works in a fast-paced open plan office and is surrounded by very ambitious people who are under a lot of pressure in very busy, target and deadline driven roles. Frankie very quickly gained the respect and trust of his peers and managers, something that in my experience is not an easy thing to do in a sales environment where people have little time to waste and are focused only on the job at hand. He is relied upon heavily by a large, growing team of consultants and has worked hard to produce very good results and is gaining positive feedback. In response to this, Frankie has been given a number of additional responsibilities, resulting in a permanent position within the business."*

Susanna concluded by saying: *"Achieving success in our business plan relies heavily on us growing our temp business – something we simply couldn't achieve without the support across compliance and finance. We look forward to investing further not only in Frankie's, but also in other apprentices' careers through MiddletonMurray moving forward."*

Speaking at the presentation of his Award when all his colleagues at Tay stood up and applauded him, Frankie said: *"Coming to Tay I knew it would be a great working environment that I would fit into. Last year I developed substantially and this is down to everyone at Tay and MiddletonMurray. I would like to say special thanks to my Director Susanna, my CEO Caroline and my assessor Jan for nominating me and for all their support and guidance over the last year. This is a great achievement and I'm very proud."*

Outstanding attitudinal qualities single out Alex for success

Apprentice of the Month –
Alex McDonnell – August 2014

A professional and confident attitude, a willingness to support her colleagues, always being punctual, regularly completing her NVQ work to a high standard and being immaculately dressed, were just some of the attributes cited by her assessor and employer which resulted in Alex McDonnell of Henry George Estates Group being named as the winner of the MiddletonMurray 'Apprentice of the Month' Award for August.

As always it was a tough decision for the judges as they were also particularly impressed by the achievements of **Pauline Meyer** of Tavistock Institute who received an excellent testimonial from her assessor. However, the judges felt that Alex was fully deserving of the Award, as explained by Angela Middleton: *"We chose Alex because of the outstanding attitudinal qualities she regularly displays which are so important and because of her clear determination to do well."*

Iza Alberdi, Alex's assessor at MiddletonMurray, pictured here with Alex at her presentation said: *"I'm delighted that Alex has won this month's Award. She always has a huge smile on her face and she completes her daily tasks and NVQ work to a consistently high standard. Alex regularly goes the extra mile when completing her work and often emails me to undertake extra assignments. Despite her young age, she comes across as a very professional and confident young lady who has also made a great impression with her management team."*

Speaking at the presentation of her Award, Alex, who has since completed her apprenticeship and is now currently applying for new positions said: *"I would like to thank MiddletonMurray for giving this Award to me, I'm very proud of myself and a special thank you to my assessor Iza for putting me forward for it and helping me through my apprenticeship.* Alex continued; *"I would now like to work on property management to utilise the skills I have gained at Henry George Estates. My aim is to manage my own portfolio of properties."*

Pam Williams, Lettings Manager at Henry George Estates Group said: *"Alex was a good team member of the group; she worked well on her own and also as part of the team. She always offered to stay late if needed and to do that little bit extra to help out. Alex was always prompt and always immaculately dressed."*

The key to Gemma's success— a sense of humour!

Apprentice of the Month –
Gemma Ives – July 2014

A strong willingness to learn, a determination to take on any task and do it to the best of her ability, the production of excellent written assignments plus an infectious sense of humour that creates a vibrant atmosphere around her; these were just some of the reasons which resulted in Gemma Ives of Schillings being named as the winner of the MiddletonMurray 'Apprentice of the Month' Award for July.

Once again, the judges had a tough task in choosing this month's winner as they were extremely impressed by the two other nominees, **Maryum Nazir,** who is currently out of placement and **Samantha Stockbridge** of Pimlico Plumbers, both of whom received outstanding testimonials from their assessors. However, the judges felt that Gemma fully deserved the Award, as explained by Peter Varney: "*We chose Gemma* *principally because she has progressed well and has a more varied workload to undertake and is clearly showing good commitment and progress."*

Patricia Peters, Gemma's assessor at MiddletonMurray said: *"Gemma has a great working relationship with her manager at Schillings and has showed herself to be a great team player who does not shy away from a challenge. Gemma's attitude to her learning is first class and she always ensures that her assignments are completed on time and welcomes feedback. Gemma is a joy to work with; she is humble and willing and eager to learn. She takes her responsibilities seriously and is determined to do a great job, no matter what the task. She also has a great sense of humour, which brings a vibrant atmosphere to her working environment. I am delighted that her progress has been recognised by the judges – she deserves this accolade."*

Martin Flowers, Gemma's Manager at Schillings said: *"Gemma is the first apprentice we've taken on at Schillings and we've been impressed with her work ethic and ability to step up and take on new tasks. Gemma is a popular member of our team and we are delighted that MiddletonMurray has recognised her hard work. Well done Gemma!"*

Speaking at the presentation of her Award, Gemma said: *"I feel that after coming into an environment I didn't know, I've really improved, but I know there is still a way to go and that winning this Award is a great achievement which will really help me to push that little bit more to get to where I want to be."*

Molly multi-tasks her way to success

Apprentice of the Month – Molly O'Neil – June 2014

An enthusiastic attitude, a willingness to learn and a strong ability to multi-task were just some of the attributes that made Molly O'Neil the stand-out winner of the MiddletonMurray 'Apprentice of the Month' Award for June, making it two wins in a row for Molly's employers, Lewisham-based CIS Security following Georgina Martin's success in winning the Award in May!

With the standard of nominations being so consistently high, the judges' decision is getting harder and harder to make and they were extremely impressed by both **Gintare Miciulyte** of First Contact and **Adam Miles** of Uplift Properties, both of whom received outstanding testimonials from their assessors and employers. However, the judges felt that Molly was fully deserving of the Award and in particular recognised her outstanding achievement in already having won CIS Security's 'Employee of the Month' accolade.

Proscovia Kasovia, Molly's assessor at MiddletonMurray said: *"Molly is always smartly dressed and professional. At my first visit I wouldn't have recognised her as an apprentice, she was so confident in managing a very busy reception area. Molly's standard of work is always high, she has strong ability to multi-task and yet still delivers high quality work. Molly's success in winning 'Employee of the Month' at CIS Security just goes to show her hard work and determination to succeed."*

Tracy Plant, HR Director at CIS Security said: *"From the outset Molly has shown keen enthusiasm to learn and has picked up all tasks given her and run with them with flying colours! Predominantly based on reception, Molly was initially a little apprehensive about being at the front of house by herself but after the first week showed tremendous confidence and now has no problem in managing our busy switchboard and her reception duties on her own, and to a high standard."*

Tracy continued: *"Molly is now an integral part of the team and is always willing to take on new challenges. She never says no to any tasks that are presented to her and her work is to a very high standard including her levels of accuracy. Molly is extremely flexible, presentable and reliable, she has a lovely personality and maintains a professional image within the office and we are delighted her efforts have been recognised by the MiddletonMurray 'Apprentice of the Month' judges."*

Speaking at the presentation of her 'Apprentice of the Month' Award, Molly said: *"I'm very pleased to have won this Award. I've received a lot of support from MiddletonMurray, my assessor Proscovia and my employers CIS Security. I'm very happy to have undertaken an apprenticeship as it showed me how to work within a professional business and it actually helped me to achieve a permanent position within CIS."*

Molly concluded by saying: *"MiddletonMurray was able to provide me with the opportunity of working in such a successful business and they showed me that if you work hard you'll achieve your goals."*

Double Award success for Georgina

Apprentice of the Month – Georgina Martin – May 2014

Being organised, very professional and dedicated to her job were some of the attributes that saw Georgina Martin win the 'Employee of the Month' Award at her employers, Lewisham-based CIS Security and now she has another award to celebrate the MiddletonMurray 'Apprentice of the Month' Award for May.

Once again the judges had a tough decision to make in choosing this month's winner as they were extremely impressed by both **Holly Martin** of Dataswift South East Ltd and **Pauline Meyer** of the Tavistock Institute, both of whom received outstanding testimonials from their assessors and employers. However, the judges felt that Georgina was fully deserving of the Award and in particular recognised her outstanding achievement in winning her company's 'Employee of the Month' accolade.

Proscovia Kasovia, Georgina's assessor at MiddletonMurray said: *"Georgina is so organised; at my visits I have been impressed by the way she operates, she is very professional and dedicated to her job. I am always pleased by the way she consistently performs in what is a very busy environment, undertaking an HR role at a level above what you'd normally expect from an apprentice."*

Proscovia continued: *"Georgina has made tremendous progress from a shy young person at our first visit to a very professional and confident young lady. Her personality has developed during her time with CIS Security and she is now a valued member of the team."*

Tracy Plant, HR Director at CIS Security said: *"Georgina conducts her work extremely effectively. She is responsible for security vetting all new starters and TUPE transfers to the business. Georgina is also recognised for her ability to communicate clearly and effectively informing all managers, some at board level, of the developments of new starters. She has developed a good rapport with all members of staff, including the Managing Director. Georgina is personable and friendly and maintains a professional image in the office and she was deservedly awarded the 'Employee of the Month' Award for her outstanding achievements, speed and accuracy."*

On hearing of her 'Apprentice of the Month' Award, Georgina said: *"I am really grateful for the opportunities and great placement which MiddletonMurray was able to provide for me. Doing my apprenticeship with MiddletonMurray and working with CIS Security has helped me become more confident and develop my skills within my role. I am very pleased with what I have achieved within CIS Security and I would not have been able to do it without MiddletonMurray and the help and support from my assessor. I am very glad that I took part in the apprenticeship programme and I would definitely recommend it to others."*

Consistent approach proves successful for Ryan

Apprentice of the Month – Ryan O'Shaughnessy – April 2014

A willingness to learn and improve plus continually projecting a positive image despite a heavy workload were some of the factors that led to Ryan O'Shaughnessy, an apprentice Estate Agent at Hunters Estate Agency, one of the UK's fastest growing independent estate agents and letting agents, being selected as the MiddletonMurray 'Apprentice of the Month' for April.

Ludlow Dixon, Ryan's assessor at MiddletonMurray said: *"Ryan consistently gets his work in when asked. There have been times when his workload has been quite heavy but he's always put in an effort to try and complete his assignment when asked and he always tries to project a positive image even when under pressure. He has a polite and helpful attitude to clients and makes them feel welcomed in the company."*

Ludlow continued: *"Ryan has developed his skills and grown within Hunters Estate Agency. He is now a valued member of the team with the ability to work in different areas of the business."*

On hearing of his Award, Ryan said: *"I feel very happy and surprised; this is a good achievement and the fact that my work has been recognised and I am receiving this Award has definitely encouraged me to work even harder."*

Once again there were some other outstanding candidates in contention and the judges had a tough choice to make. MiddletonMurray CEO Angela Middleton, who chairs the judging panel said: *"It was certainly a tricky one this month! However we chose Ryan because of his ongoing consistency despite a very heavy workload at times. Sometimes the consistent performers who don't cause any issues and who quietly tackle their challenges can go unnoticed — the unsung heroes as it were! So although we were extremely impressed by the other nominees we decided that Ryan thoroughly deserved the Award this month."*

Maths + Confidence = Success for Sibel

Apprentice of the Month – Sibel Kasab – March 2014

A confidence in Mathematics and being able to work independently and autonomously were attributes cited by her assessor and her manager for Sibel Kasab's achievement in being chosen as the MiddletonMurray 'Apprentice of the Month' for March.

Tony Withers, MiddletonMurray's internal verifier and lead assessor said: "*I am delighted that Sibel, an Apprentice Administrator at APSCo, has been selected as our 'Apprentice of the Month'. She has provided one of the highest standards of assessment evidence I have received by a candidate. She works independently and autonomously in her job, and has taken on responsibilities beyond a typical administrator's role. She has a bright and positive outlook on both employment and study and can balance, in a mature way, her priorities. She has gone from strength to strength in her NVQ delivery, but what has impressed me the most is her confidence in Mathematics.*"

"*I recently had a review with Sibel and her manager Fiona Lander,*" continued Tony: "*and Fiona spoke very highly of Sibel, and will be offering her a job. We all discussed the prospects of Sibel doing the Level 3 in Business and Administration, and to APSCo's credit, they will fully support this. This to me indicates a valued employee who has worked hard to gain both a job and further training.*"

Speaking after hearing the news of her success, Sibel said: "*I feel privileged that my hard work has been acknowledged. Receiving this recognition has encouraged me to do even more and develop further skills. I am now looking forward to starting a Level 3 qualification at the end of this current one!*"

'Apprentice of the Month' judge Tessa Oversby said: "*My fellow judges and I all agree that Sibel Kasab was an outstanding candidate this month – she has a good commitment to both studying and the job role, which has been rewarded by her being offered a permanent role at APSCo.*"

Confidence Boost for Ellen

Apprentice of the Month –
Ellen Blood – February 2014

Running the office on her own and pushing herself beyond her comfort zone were two of the factors why Ellen Blood, an Administrative Assistant at the Children's Heart Federation was the stand-out candidate for the MiddletonMurray 'Apprentice of the Month' Award for February.

Iza Alberdi, Ellen's assessor at MiddletonMurray said: *"Ellen has an extremely proactive attitude towards her work and qualifications. She impressed me greatly when arranging a presentation in the company's boardroom on the day of my visit. She always produces work of a very high quality and she tries her best on every single task assigned to her. Despite her young age, she comes across as a very professional and confident young lady."*

Kate Smith, Ellen's Manager at the Children's Heart Federation said: *"Ellen is an integral part of our team. She is a hard worker and quick to learn. We have a very small and very busy office and she has slotted into it perfectly. She has taken on many roles in her short time of being here and when I am out of the office or away on annual leave I am confident that she can run things in my absence. She not only assists me but every other member of our team and all the departments. I receive great praise from my other staff members about her work. She is very young but her age is not important because her maturity is so impressive."*

Kate continued: *"Ellen sometimes lacks confidence when talking to people, either on the phone or in person. However she has tackled this by making sure she picks up every phone call and even though she isn't comfortable talking to a meeting room full of people she still goes in and does it. Ellen did some research for our Family Support Department and presented it to our Chief Executive and our Operations Manager – both were very impressed by the work she did and how she carried it out. I can see her confidence building daily and it is lovely to watch. She will continue to be a very important part of this team."*

'Apprentice of the Month' judge Peter Varney said: *"I loved the report on Ellen. Even though it has only been four months, the fact she offers to do extra hours at weekends and that she can be left to run the office on her own already displays all the qualities you seek in an apprentice. She also is prepared to take on interfacing with other more senior people in the organisation even though she lacks confidence, but that is the best way to build confidence and she has clearly grasped that already."*

Full Steam Ahead for Alfie

Apprentice of the Month –
Alfie Witsey – January 2014

Attention to detail and always being ready to take on new challenges were just two of the factors that led to Alfie Witsey, an Administrative Assistant at Southeastern Railway being unanimously selected as the MiddletonMurray 'Apprentice of the Month' for January.

Ludlow Dixon, Alfie Witsey's assessor at MiddletonMurray said: *"Alfie has always produced his work with attention to detail and he has worked conscientiously in his placement, so much so that he is now being offered a contract. I spoke with his manager who was impressed with Alfie and explained that the plan is for him to progress into a more developmental role."*

Harry Persaud, Recruitment Manager, Southeastern, said: *"It has been a pleasure working with Alfie, his performance with the Recruitment team has been outstanding, so much so that we have extended his contract for another year."* Harry continued; *"I have always found Alfie very helpful and he is very much liked by all the team members. One of his greatest strengths is that he is always ready to take on a new challenge. He has proved invaluable with the work he has done so far within the department."*

Once again there were some other outstanding candidates in contention but the panel were in total agreement in their selection for the January Award. Peter Varney said: *"The ultimate test is are they being offered a permanent position and clearly Alfie has impressed Southeastern Railway to such an extent that they have offered him a contract after just six months and have already identified the area of the business that they want him to concentrate on."*

On hearing of his Award, Alfie from Orpington, Kent said: *"I am forever grateful for the opportunities that were presented to me at MiddletonMurray and the apprenticeship placement that they managed to find for me. They have helped me develop my skills and help me reach my full potential. My confidence has grown throughout my placement to a level which I didn't believe was in me. My assessor has supported me immensely and has helped me in many aspects of my apprenticeship. I have come on leaps and bounds, and I believe that the qualification that I gain at the end of my apprenticeship will help me in any career that I wish to pursue in the years ahead. I am delighted to have won 'Apprentice of the Month' and I am glad that my hard work is paying off."*

Positive attitude the key to success for Lucy

Apprentice of the Month – Lucy Street – December 2013

A positive attitude to her work and to her studies were just two of the attributes that led to Lucy Street of Insurance Brokers Bellegrove Insurance being unanimously selected as the MiddletonMurray 'Apprentice of the Month' for December.

Ludlow Dixon, Lucy Street's assessor at MiddletonMurray said: *"Lucy's attitude to attendance for assessment meetings and getting assignments completed as requested is first class and she is well on the way to completion of the Business Administration course. She is extremely positive and works hard to make assessment meetings enjoyable. She began working as an administration assistant but such was her performance and her respect for colleagues that she has been given a contract by Bellegrove Insurance before the end of her apprenticeship placement."*

Whilst there were some outstanding other candidates, the Awards panel were unanimous in their selection for the December

Award. Steve Sutherland said: *"I think all of the nominated apprentices have clearly performed extremely well but for me Lucy Street stands out, simply because of the fact that she has so impressed her employer and her colleagues that she has been given a contract before the end of her apprenticeship placement. Surely, you can't really do better than that!"*

Tessa Oversby, Head of Employability, UK Retail & Business Banking, Barclays Bank Plc said: *"I really love the approach, behaviours and attitude of the other nominees but, like Steve, my vote for this month goes to Lucy for being 'first class' all round and earning a permanent contract before her apprenticeship had even ended!"*

This was also the clincher for Peter Varney, the CEO of KEH Sports Ltd and Vice Chairman of Ebbsfleet United FC who said: *"All of the nominees have excellent feedback but the real test is always has the person done so well they are taken on. In Lucy Street's case she has been given a permanent role early and given client accounts to manage so where the selection of the winner is so close, as in this case, this tips the balance for me."*

MiddletonMurray CEO Angela Middleton spoke of the high standards set by Lucy's employers: *"I am delighted that Lucy has been chosen and I know she certainly will be! Bellegrove Insurance operates within a very competitive environment and has very high standards so the fact they gave Lucy a permanent role so quickly speaks volumes."*

On hearing of her success, Lucy Street said: *"I started my apprenticeship nearly a year ago and in this time I have gained many new skills and secured a permanent job. I believe the biggest benefit from doing an apprenticeship is that it helps you to get experience working in an office, which many young people struggle to get. My assessor has been brilliant and made sure I never have any problems in my placement as well as supporting me with my coursework. I have enjoyed my apprenticeship and would recommend it to anyone."*

About The Author

Angela Middleton was born in Deptford, south-east London. The eldest of three children, her father was a roofer and her mum worked in a bakery. A quiet, shy but diligent child, she attended some tough inner London schools before her family moved to Sidcup in Kent where she attended Blackfen School for Girls, achieving three GCSE A Levels. Despite minimal careers guidance she secured her first job with BP Oil as a management trainee in an office full of men. Apprehensive, full of insecurities and unaware of her potential, she quietly observed the behaviour of her successful colleagues and copied them until she felt more confident. She was the first person in her family to complete a degree (Business Studies) and went on to manage departments of up to 200 people before starting MiddletonMurray. She lives with her husband and two dogs in Chislehurst, Kent and enjoys spending time with her two grown-up children who inspired her to help young people fulfil their career ambitions and to write this first book. She has a firm belief that no one needs to be unemployed and anyone can achieve their career ambitions if they want to and are prepared to work hard.